Mother Love

Portraits of its Power

Elizabeth
Adam

Cover and text design by Karen Armstrong Graphic Design, Winnipeg
Printed by Friesens, Winnipeg, Manitoba, Canada

Library and Archives Canada Cataloguing in Publication

Adam, Elizabeth, 1971-

Mother love : portraits of its power / Elizabeth Adam.

Includes bibliographical references.

ISBN 978-0-9784978-0-4

1. Love, Maternal. 2. Motherhood. I. Title.

HQ759.A33 2008 306.874'3 C2007-907245-3

To the
Giver of Life

Acknowledgements

To the Author of All – I owe everything to You.

I would like to thank my husband Herb for his faithful long-term support – spiritual, emotional, practical, and financial. I could not do this or anything else without you. I am so thankful to have you as a partner and a best friend.

Thank you to our children – for bringing mother love into my heart, for caring about me and my work, and for letting me play on the computer.

Thank you to all of my family and friends who have encouraged me and cared about my as-yet-invisible writing pursuits.

Deniece Reimer – Thank you for editing this manuscript late at night in the midst of toilet training your daughter!

Lois Crockford – Thank you for everything you have done and will do to support me and this work, but especially I thank you for letting me adopt you—now I know a lot more about love.

Thank you to the twelve wonderful women* who shared their stories so openly and honestly for this book. In many cases, these stories were hard to tell. Thank you for opening your hearts for us, even when that was painful. You have enriched us all.

**For privacy or legal purposes, some of the women whose stories are told have chosen to use pseudonyms.*

Mother Love
Portraits of its Power

Preface

Is it possible to portray the power of mother love? Can anyone describe exactly what happens to a woman when she becomes a mother—when she is baptized with this fire that heats her heart and warms those around her?

The transformation, the passion, the pain, the joy, the meaning of mother love—we can't explain these things let alone express them. When I was interviewing women for this book I kept hearing phrases like "I can't put it into words" or "There are no words for it"; but I somehow understood what the mothers were trying to say. I could feel the strains of their hearts as they struggled to express things deep inside of them. It wasn't until later that I realized I wouldn't be able to fully put the depth of their experiences and emotions into words for them.

Even though this book presents my perspective on other peoples' stories, and my own stories, it isn't really about me. It is about all of us, and about the love that is bigger than us all.

Chapter One

Being Birthed

When does a woman become a mother? Is it when she begins to suspect or hope she might be pregnant, or maybe when she first feels bubbling flutters from within? Perhaps it's when she first lays eyes on a child she is embracing as her very own, or when an infant is laid on her chest, wet and screaming. Or does our mother love implant long before any of these sorts of things happen?

I would venture a guess that all of us, if we really looked back, could see seeds of mother love planted into us years before we officially became mothers. As much as we are prepared (or unprepared) for becoming mothers, the birth or adoption of a child ushers in not only an entirely new life and lifestyle, but a new state of being. It is an indescribable sort of change, not something a woman can really explain or even understand. Mother love is intensely heart-altering. The phrase "stretch marks on my heart" pops up now and then, which suggests a sort of damage or unattractiveness, or a shrinking after an intense swelling. I think mother love enlarges our hearts without hurting them. It makes us stronger, sweeter, more capable of love, and more beautiful in love.

Motherhood's alterations can be painful when they allow buried pain to seep out, or when they force someone erstwhile selfish to serve someone helpless. Motherhood's alterations can also be welcome, joyful, poignant, and fulfilling. I think most mothers experience both the cutting and the hemming sorts of alterations as the power of the love woven into us does its work.

When I married Herb when he was thirty-one and I was twenty, I was still a girl. Because Herb is both easy-going and sacrificial, I remained a girl until Timothy came into our lives three and half years later. The suffering I went through during pregnancy, birth, and post-partum ignited a process of maturing I didn't know I needed. It is a good thing we did not have to wait for the conception of our first child. Herb, significantly more patient by nature, would have been fine. I would not have. When I found out I was pregnant as soon as I'd planned to be I bounced about for a number of days, blissfully ignorant of the volcano about to erupt. By the time I was six weeks pregnant (four, if you're interested in being accurate) I was violently ill. After a few days of not being able to stop throwing up I got worried when I started puking green (this is the correct medical term I'm sure). I had Herb take me into the hospital where I sat for several hours in a wheelchair holding an ice-cream pail on my lap before getting sent home without being miraculously and instantly cured as I'd expected to be.

The prescription I got didn't seem to help at all, nor did the ancient "eat two crackers before rising" advice—they just came right back up as did almost everything else. The next number of months felt like forever. I threw up more than I thought was really possible, but did live to tell about it. I'm not sure, though, if there's much to tell about vomiting that could be considered meaningful. I have quite a number of very vivid morning sickness memories I could share, none of which are particularly inspirational, so I will simply summarize this difficult period of time with a piece of advice to anyone who may be currently suffering the same sort of situation—try not to throw up upwind.

When the puking was mostly past, I was able to have an ultrasound. I had to cancel a previous appointment because I knew I would never be able to keep the water down. We didn't get a picture to take home but I can still remember the image of the baby inside me, fully formed, strong of heart and backbone. Though I was quite aware I was pregnant, this being that was supposedly living inside of me seemed unreal. When you're pregnant or waiting for an adoption, the child you await is a great unknown. You can feel the child inside you and maybe even know what gender it will be. You may have seen a picture of the child that will become yours, or know his name, but until you actually get to know the child, he is mostly a mystery.

Shortly after giving birth to Timothy I perched uncomfortably on the edge of a hard hospital bed beside the being that had come out of my womb into the world. Once a mystery, he was now a wonder to me, lying in a bassinette encased in a standard white hospital bundling system. The baby looked exactly as I'd expected him to look—dark hair, blue eyes, and an average size, yet I was somehow surprised. This was a real person here! The hair, the fingernails, the lips. . . could this have been inside of me?

When a nurse wheeled me from the delivery room to the room I'd be staying in she noticed I was crying and asked if I was in pain. I was in pain, but that was not why I was crying. I wondered what could be wrong with the nurse. Was it not obvious that I had just given birth to the most beautiful child ever born? Who wouldn't cry? Had I been in any sort of state to think rationally, I would have taken into account the fact that these nurses see dozens of babies on a daily basis. Not to mention the fact that my awarding the "Most Beautiful Baby Ever Born" title might be rather biased, but I was thinking with my heart at that particular moment instead of my head. We need those sorts of thoughts sometimes.

I found out pretty quickly that I was rather uninformed about how to take care of this unpredictable bundle despite my preparatory reading. I had done some babysitting as a teenager and even had a part-time job taking care of three small children not long before Timothy was born but I had never had any close contact with a brand-new baby. I couldn't get his sharp little nails cut. I didn't know how to go about changing his diaper, which seems silly now, and I found out that breast-feeding was far more challenging than I ever thought it could be. Before I had a baby I would inwardly raise my eyebrows at friends who attended breastfeeding support groups and took sessions on things like problem solving in the nursing relationship. "Breast – mouth," I would think, "How difficult can it be?" I found out the hard way that it can actually be very difficult, not for every mother but for some, and I was one of the some.

Timothy's first night in the hospital must have gone well. A nurse told me he was the best baby in the nursery, and I felt proud for no reason whatsoever. The second night he was obviously not the best baby in the nursery and got shipped off to me in the wee hours that seem to be designed for dealing with wee ones. I did not know quite what to do with him other than walk around with him, so I picked him up and painfully walked around the room, bracing myself against a wall after a while so I didn't fall over.

Some time ago I sat with an adoptive mother at a conference lunch. She told me how she and her husband felt a little awkward during the early days with their new baby. They had to get used to the fact that they were her parents. When their new baby would cry they would tell themselves, "Well, she's ours. I guess we'll pick her up." I assured her that those are the same sort of thoughts birth parents have. Something as life altering as a new life to look after takes a bit of getting used to.

Somehow, I learned how to understand and care for this child who had come so wondrously into our world. It wasn't long before I felt I knew Timothy very deeply, and that I was uniquely his mother. When Tim was about four months old we were visited by my Kenyan friend Ann and her mother. When Kenyan women become mothers they take on the name of their oldest child. MamaAnn lay little Timothy down along on her lap with the comfort of much experience and gazed down at him. "What does your Mama do to make you laugh?" she asked him. And by then, I knew.

I was crazy about this child before I even conceived him, and strongly attached as soon as I set my hand on his heart when he was placed on my chest right after birth. Yet, there was a sort of distance between us in the early days despite our constant closeness. When Timothy was very new a friend said to me, "In a month or so you'll be so bonded to the little guy." I was sure I already was but then a day came when I found myself crying simply because I loved him so much. I cannot remember precisely what I was thinking but I knew something significant had happened inside. My son had gone from being a fantasy, to a reality, to an integral part of my heart. Love for him will live within me as long as I live.

Twelve years have passed since I carried him inside my body. Somehow, both gradually and rapidly, he has changed from a bundle in my arms to a boy who can carry me on his back. The bond between us has changed colors from the intense scarlet born of pain and deep need, to the sunshiny yellow a bright-eyed preschooler emits, to a very deep blue reflecting the oceans of time we have spent together, and the depths of our affection for each other. No matter what color our relationship is on any given day, I know it will endure all the way to eternity, and that I will always love this child no matter what he does or doesn't do.

One bright fall day when Timmy, as we called him then, was four years old we sat together on a riverbank watching the water flow. He was wearing his favorite orange fleece jacket with teddy bears on it. Out of the blue Timmy said to me, "I want to be four forever. And I want you to be … How old are you?"

"Twenty-eight," I told him.

"I want you to be twenty-eight forever."

Most people have moments when they wish time would stand still. This was one of them for me; but time doesn't ever stand still. It keeps moving whether we want it to or not. That constant motion is what forces us forward and upward, creating growth as it goes. The orange jacket doesn't fit Tim anymore, and I don't think he would want it to.

"Where do the years go?" a friend asked recently as we talked about how her once freckle-faced toddler will be graduating from high school soon. I do not know where years go. I only know that they go quickly, if not while they are passing then certainly after they have passed. I think back to Timothy's babyhood with a heart-squeezing sort of sentiment. Baby Timothy lives only in my memory now. I cannot hold him anymore. I cannot even see him since the pictures do not do him justice. But Timothy my son is still here to love, even if he won't let me kiss him anymore.

When I was thinking about writing this chapter I looked through an album of Tim's baby year and came across a picture of me holding him when he was just a few months old. I remember being weary in every way when that picture was taken, but I look so young—fresh-faced and wide-eyed. There is no trace of the crinkles I now display, whether I want to or not.

I do not wish I could go back to being fresh-faced and wide-eyed—I am much better now than I was then—but I do wish I could have had the wisdom and the perspective back then that my years of mothering have given me. I guess it can't really work that way, so I will just be thankful for the lessons I have learned and the transformations that have taken place. Each of the 4500 or so days I have logged as a mother are significant—the difficult, the dreary, and the delightful. I am counting each one as a gift.

Richelle's Story

Richelle left her mother when she was twelve years old. She simply couldn't endure her mother's abuse any longer and she was old enough, in the tragic world she grew up in, to live in the hotels on Hastings Street in downtown Vancouver. "I have vague memories of my mother on the floor with bruises," Richelle told me over coffee one night, trying to make sense of why her mother treated her six children the way she did.

Richelle is the fifth of six siblings, each from a different father. Before Richelle was born her oldest sister was raped and murdered at just six years old. Right around the time of her daughter's horrific death, Richelle's mother Thelma also lost her mother and her husband. Unable to process these disastrous losses and almost certainly the victim of abuse herself, Thelma became violently abusive toward her children, and desperately addicted to alcohol and drugs.

The children soon came to realize that if their mother didn't get enough pot, they would be in trouble. Thelma would beat them with hockey sticks, bang their heads together, yank their hair, or give them black eyes or a broken nose. "You never knew what to expect," Richelle said. When I asked her if there was ever a time she remembered her mother making an effort to be kind or trying to clean herself up, it didn't take her long to answer, "No."

From time to time Child and Family Services workers would check on the family and Thelma would somehow know exactly what to say and how to say it in order to pull the wool over the social workers' eyes and blind them to the incredible abuses that she was regularly inflicting on her children. Later in life, Richelle had to fight the system to get her sister's and her cousin's children removed from her mother's home, which further strained family relationships.

As a result of the abuse and neglect she was suffering, Richelle had difficulty concentrating in school. After finishing grade seven she gave up on school and turned to selling pot to keep herself alive. Pot was a good thing for her to sell since she didn't like it, but she did use alcohol and other drugs. "I've pretty much done everything," she told me in a tired sort of voice. "There had to be drama or I had to create it."

Richelle began an on and off relationship with a guy from the street whose only good quality was that he was good-looking. Right after she turned sixteen she found out she was pregnant. Even though she was never careful with birth control she felt shocked. She tried to establish a permanent relationship with the father of her child but he pushed and kicked her during her pregnancy, and punched her in the jaw.

"I didn't want my baby to grow up with this violent person," she told me over one of our coffee dates. "If he hit me when I was pregnant, what would he do with the child?" Before the baby was born, a SWAT team was sent to the place they were living in and her boyfriend was taken away on theft charges. He was found guilty by the courts and jailed for robbing banks and a jewellery store.

I asked Richelle if she ever thought of aborting the baby. "I just didn't think it was right," she answered, "I just knew I was having a baby, that I was going to be a mother." In time, Richelle gave birth to a little boy she named Alec. Alone in her room, she asked to see him and after being wheeled to the nursery Richelle sat beside her baby, gazing into the bassinette that held her son. It was then that something happened deep on the inside of her, where nothing had ever touched her before. She reached inside the transparent walls that surrounded her baby and took his tiny hand in hers. And she decided she would change. For the sake of this child, she would do everything she could to change.

"It's a feeling that you've never had—I can't really explain it. It's a miracle." It is always a miracle when a mother is born. Sometimes that miracle doesn't take root, or is somehow stomped upon or ripped out, but in Richelle the miracle flourished and gave her the footholds she needed to climb out of the world she was born into.

Being a young teenaged mother with nowhere to live, a newborn baby to care for, and a seventh grade education, Richelle was not a likely candidate to be able to free herself from the addictions she had already developed before her pregnancy began. While she was pregnant, Richelle found it fairly easy not to use drugs or alcohol because the baby inside provided the incentive she needed but after the baby was born, the physical and emotional cravings returned. Richelle fought her battles alone, without support from family, friends, or any organizations and was miraculously able to become completely free from drug and alcohol use even while still living in places where they were being used all the time.

Richelle took Baby Alec to see his birthfather in jail once, and sent a few pictures. That was the only contact between them until several years later when Alec's father was out of jail and called Richelle to try to get back together with her. Fortunately, Richelle had long since moved on and up. Because he was such a violent person and seemed to be continuing his pre-prison life, Richelle wonders whether he is even still alive.

Richelle lived with her mother for a short time after giving birth but hated being around her mother's "lunatic behavior" when she would get in a rage and lose control. Richelle escaped with her baby and moved in with her older sister. It was there that she first met Steve, an acquaintance of her sister's. Steve was twenty-six years old and not managing his life well at the time. When he met Richelle, just sixteen years old with a baby to care for, he was impressed with the way she was working to make a better life for herself and her son. Steve began to reconsider his own choices, especially when he noticed the difference between his childhood and hers.

It took a while for Richelle to allow herself to like Steve, but they began a relationship with each other after a few months. They had a son they named Jordan together almost two years after Alec's birth and got married about a year later. A few months into their marriage they thought it might be nice to have a little girl and before they could change their minds Richelle became pregnant—with two girls.

When Richelle went in for a routine ultrasound, the technician told her she had two babies inside of her. Richelle started to cry, overwhelmed at the very possibility. She felt both very happy and very scared at the same time. The concept of having twins was unbelievable to her, and she wondered if she could even carry two babies let alone take care of them and their two older brothers.

Richelle was able to carry the twins up until 32 weeks gestation when Quianna and Brittney were born almost two months early weighing 4'6" and 5'3". After delivering Quianna, Richelle's heart began to fluctuate rapidly. "Take the baby," she told the nurses, "I can't breathe." A code blue was called out and the delivery room remained extremely tense until doctors intervened to help deliver Brittney from a breech position and Richelle's heart could be stabilized.

Mother and babies recuperated from the birth well and Richelle was able to get a little help in the home from a government program after the girls first came home. They were beautiful babies—one dark like her mother, one fair like her father. Life moved into a new sort of normal, a much busier one. But it was not long until another major adjustment appeared on the horizon – a surprise pregnancy discovered when the twins were still babies. By the time they were 18 months old they had a baby sister. Richelle had her hands and her house very full.

"I always want to do better," Richelle said to me. "I feel like there's not enough time for the five of them." Personally, I feel she is doing extraordinarily and miraculously well. I like her laugh, and the way her eyes smile at her children. Richelle's mothering defies explanation. She carries out none of her mother's rages against her own children, somehow evading the powerful force of patterning. Richelle is immensely calm in the midst of the clamor of five growing children living in one half of a side-by-side. She is gentle and generous with her children and deeply tenderhearted over not only her own children but many others as well. She cares profoundly for Steve's two older sons from his first marriage. She has long talks over the telephone with the older son, trying to help him sort out his life, and has warmly welcomed the younger son into the family for long periods of time when he wasn't willing or able to live with his mother.

Richelle volunteers with our children's church program sometimes. It is sweet for me to see her children following her around like magnets, resting their faces on her arm. Steve and Richelle often let their kids each have a friend over to play, doubling the household head count and noise levels. Richelle takes people in even though they are already cramped for space, and is the only person I know who gives her husband's ex-wife a place to stay when she needs one.

Richelle's mother used to call her children "bitches", "sluts", "stupid", and "good for nothing", and Richelle is not completely free from all the effects of her mother's emotional and physical abuse. She finds schoolwork difficult but is working valiantly at finishing her high school diploma a course at a time. She dreams of possibly going into social work someday where she would be able to rescue the children stuck in the sorts of situations she had to grow up in. Unlike workers observing from the outside, she feels she would be able to tell when a parent was covering up abuse.

Richelle sometimes feels almost overwhelmingly sad, especially when she thinks about how most of her relatives are still living the life she's been able to escape. Richelle knows how close she came to living the life she was born into. "The only reason I chose differently is because I had Alec," she states. That choice was not an easy one to carry out on her own, but she's persevered and is giving her children the gift of a much better childhood than she had.

Richelle is a remarkably strong woman, persevering through physical and emotional exhaustion, financial strains, chronic lower back pain, and the ever-present responsibilities of raising five children. When the children were very young, she was able to care for them at home until Steve was injured in a construction accident and became unable to work. The last number of years, Richelle has been working to keep their family afloat financially. She has worked full-time at a used clothing store as well as doing custodial work for a private school. She's now doing custodial work at a university and Steve is retraining for a non-construction job now that the children are all in school.

I felt quite surprised the day Richelle told me she wanted more babies and that she and Steve were thinking about having her tubal ligation reversed. As I looked at the facts later—I could see where she was coming from. She had five babies in five years. She had barely turned 22 when she had her last one. She is still young, she loves babies and children, and she probably wants a chance to do it all over again now that the whirlwind has sort of blown over. I think she knows the thought of having more children isn't particularly practical, but Richelle isn't enslaved by practicalities the way so many of us are. She does what she needs to do and spares herself the over-analyzing. "I would rather live in a grass hut eating ants with my family than be rich and alone," she told me once.

Truth be told, Richelle is actually very rich—in love, in grace, in perseverance, in compassion, and in children—all of which are far greater treasures than anything money can buy.

On Waiting and Wondering

About thirty years ago feminist Adrienne Rich stated, "Women have always been seen as waiting: waiting to be asked, waiting for our menses, in fear lest they do or do not come, waiting for men to come home from wars, or from work, waiting for children to grow up, or for the birth of a new child, or for menopause."[1] I'm not sure if Rich was saying that women have come out of our waiting roles; but if she was, I think she was wrong. We still have to wait. And we still hate to wait.

Even if we were not impatient by nature, the lack of control that waiting implies can squeeze our spirits and our self-worth. Sometimes when I am being completely ignored by someone who is supposed to be waiting on me in a store I find myself wondering, "Am I invisible?" I don't think women are the only human beings who suffer the effects of having to wait for something we want. We all have to wait in lines at banks and stores, for tickets or fast food, for attention at a doctor's office, for attention from Mommy, for friends to show up, for food to cook, or for a job or a mate to come around. When you're standing at a counter waiting for something, you always have the option of waving your arms and yelling. When you're waiting for something like a marriage partner, or a baby, that doesn't work so well.

The Western world's standard for child spacing seems to be about two years. Of course, there are many exceptions to this rule that happen either on purpose or by "accident", but two years seems to be our society's customary norm. Accepting social law without question, Herb and I planned to have our children two years apart. Assuming conception would occur as immediately as it did the first time, I had everything planned precisely including exactly how many days I had left to get things done before sickness would hit at five and a half weeks. When my period came hard and heavy that very first "trying" cycle, I was initiated into the sad, secret land of the infertile where the future is unknown and uncontrollable. A friend who suffered a bad bout of waiting for a child once told me, "It's like having a death in the family every month," and I soon came to understand what she meant.

Just this afternoon I flipped a page of a quote calendar and smiled when I read, "In waiting we begin to get in touch with the rhythms of life…." I am quite sure that Richard Foster was not thinking about menstrual cycles when he wrote this, but it reminded me of how women who are trying to get pregnant become very aware of their "rhythms of life"; living in two week increments, seeking intently to discern the drop of an invisible egg, then constantly checking for signs of life.

When Tim was quite little, barely talking, he crawled up into my lap one day and commented choppily, "Timmy has no brothers or sisters yet. Too bad." I thought this was a strange thing for such a young child to say, but he kept on asking for a sibling for years. One morning as I was lifting Tim up onto the kitchen counter to "help" make breakfast he asked me, "Where's my sister?" I can't remember what I said. I didn't know. Fertility is a terrible thing to lose. Because of my mother's history of repeated miscarriages, I had some vague notion I might have trouble having a baby but when our first baby was conceived and carried to term exactly as planned, I put this thought out of my mind and took fertility for granted the same way most people do.

As hope and disappointment began to cycle, my wondering began to become worrying mixed with strong doses of frustration and despair. The emotional suffering was deep and lonely, and accentuated with physical suffering. I ended up having three surgeries in eighteen months. Periods after surgery feel like labor, and periods during this time of my life brought two types of pain, both physical and emotional. I was sick of seeing one-lined tests, and I despaired of ever being able to turn a pregnancy test positive again. Every time there was a light or a late cycle, my hopes rose higher and fell further. One morning, I believe it was our anniversary, I had just failed another test before taking Timmy into bed with me to read some books. He noticed a tear running down my cheek and asked, "What's that Mommy?" Then he answered himself, "I think it's juice."

On one of my birthdays during my waiting and wondering years, I ended up in Emergency, which is not my choice of celebratory locales. I will not bore you with almost four years worth of medical details. I will simply summarize by stating that by the time my surgeries were over I had nine incisions in my belly. Since I would never have been caught dead in a bikini either before or after surgeries and childbearing, I can't say my bikini days are over—I never had any. I received rather a number of hospital wristbands during this season of my life. I cut one off and taped it into my memory album, making a little note beside it: "So many of these lately. I hope the next one I wear is for a good reason."

Strange as it sounds, I do have some sweet memories from this sorrowful period of time. One of my outstanding hospital memoirs is of getting toast the morning after one of my surgeries, and a jar of apple juice that I got to drink all by myself. The toast was the best toast I've ever tasted because it was still warm. This may seem like a stupid sort of memory to non-mothers, but those who have had children know that getting to eat or drink anything warm is a blessing to be appreciated. I also liked having Herb and Timmy come and see me. And I got a kick out of the older lady a few bays down who asked her visitors, "Do you want to see my boobies?" (I'm thinking she meant boo-boos.)

People who have had tumors removed and are awaiting word as to whether they are malignant or not say it is the not knowing that is the worst. Thankfully, I have not had to deal with this far more agonizing situation, but I can understand what they mean. There is tension involved with seeing two drastically different futures and not knowing which one to prepare yourself for. One thing I found hard was packing away clothes Timmy had outgrown and wondering if we would ever use them again or if I would have to give them away.

I know people struggling with the sorrow and heartbreak of infertility who have had people say things to them like, "You're not trying hard enough", "You need to go on vacation", or "You're too stressed about it–just relax." (This last piece of advice is refuted by the fact that stressed-out teen-agers and women who are raped get pregnant. The first two are just plain painful.) It also seems that some people feel the need to remind couples to have children despite the fact that even the most disorganized of couples are unlikely to forget to have a child.

We hadn't forgotten about having a second child. Though we both retreated at times into our own forms of denial—Herb that anything was really wrong, me that I didn't want another baby right now anyway—we knew what we wanted and we knew we weren't getting it. Even surgery with an extra-special doctor complete with ovarian drilling didn't do the trick. I have never been nervous about having surgery but I felt very vulnerable right before my last one when they stuck me on a steel operating table wearing only a thin gown which I knew they would take off right away and asked me where I was feeling pain in my ovary. I showed them and they marked it with an X. I found this rather unnerving.

Actually, I was more unnerved by the questions people would sometimes ask. It has ceased to amaze me how people who barely know you ask really personal questions: Are you going to have more kids? Are you trying? Are you using fertility drugs? I always appreciated the fact that both sets of our parents (if anyone has a right to ask these types of things it would be parents) did not ask these sorts of questions. I cannot say the same for some other members of the general population. Now that I look back on it, I don't know why it was me who felt uncomfortable when people asked questions that weren't their business. It's funny how we think we need to answer every question we're asked, like it's some sort of law.

I find it interesting to look back over certain time periods and see how drastically life has changed. One evening Herb, Timmy, and I went out for supper to the same restaurant Herb and I had our first date in. I thought, "Wouldn't it have been strange to look around this corner back then and see the three of us sitting here together?" Herb is too left-brained for these sorts of musings, but sometimes I wonder what it would be like to see a picture of us five or ten years down the road and try to figure out all the things that had happened during those years.

When I was in high school I went to a youth retreat where the leaders told us to write down what we thought our lives would be like in ten years, seal it in an envelope, and open it in ten years. Almost twenty years have passed since that time. I haven't opened the envelope yet, mainly because it is stuffed away in a box somewhere and I don't feel like digging around for it, but I can remember a fair bit of what I wrote. I am sure glad things didn't work out the way I wanted them to back then.

We see so dimly–and not just when we are teen-agers. Even as we become increasingly mature throughout our years, our understandings remain incomplete and our sight remains rather short. We wonder and worry about things that God already has all figured out and fixed. Gaining even one glimpse of an eternal perspective enables us to wait in peace, knowing someone sees a bigger and better picture.

Cherise's Story

Cherise is one of those socially quiet people whose depths and heights go largely unnoticed, appreciated only by those who get to see more than meets the public eye. Though she tends to become progressively quieter as the size of a group increases, Cherise is not particularly shy, and when something needs to be said she will say it. Even as a kindergarten child Cherise displayed great strength of character and commitment, purposefully going against her alcoholic father's wishes by sneaking out of her house to attend church with a friend from school.

Cherise has suffered a great deal with severe eczema and allergies since her early childhood. Many times, her eczema became so bad that she had no skin left and had to be hospitalized. Despite the fact that Cherise can rarely eat anything at restaurants or social gatherings since she is very allergic to wheat, milk, nuts, citrus, corn, and other things too numerous to mention, I have never heard her complain or indulge in the self-pity that would be the natural reaction to several of her life situations. She concentrates on the things she can eat instead of the things she can't, on the things she is thankful for instead of the things she doesn't have, on the joyful things in her life instead of the painful. She lifts her eyes from her own surroundings to see others who suffer, weeping and grieving for them over the top of her own pain.

When she was just barely twenty years old, Cherise married a young man she met at college who became emotionally abusive shortly after they were married. She endured his cruel treatment for almost three years before she decided she simply could not go on living with him any longer. The straw that broke her back occurred when they were moving, at her husband's initiation, and Cherise was expected to do all the packing and unpacking. She had just found out she was pregnant but fell and landed on the box she was carrying, which caused her to lose the baby. The way she was treated when she tried to tell her husband about the miscarriage compelled her to make a decision she never thought she would ever make. Initiating a divorce went against everything Cherise believed and felt about marriage. She realized she had done what she needed to do, yet she grieved deeply over having to do it, and at the bleak-looking future she faced.

Living with an emotionally abusive husband left Cherise's sense of self in shreds. Before she made the decision to end her marriage she was often in tears, depressed, hopeless, lonely, and abandoned. After making the decision to end her marriage, it took time for the weeds that had been planted in her heart to be removed and replaced with the fruit and the flowers that flourish there today.

By sheer spiritual strength, Cherise has been able to walk triumphantly through her life, consistently picking herself up and carrying on. About a year after her abusive marriage ended Cherise began to date Theodore, whom she met through mutual friends and eventually married. She calls him her "gift". Theodore is everything her first husband wasn't–supportive, stable, kind, faithful, and loving. They bought a home together and made plans to start a family without much delay.

Month after month began to go by. Cherise sought medical help for infertility but was told there wasn't anything to worry about. More months went by. Then the months turned into years.

Doctors began to believe Cherise's concerns, but weren't able to fix them. After nearly seven years of waiting for children, Theodore suggested trying in vitro fertilization. In vitro fertilization can be an intense, long-term medical process requiring hormone treatments and several other procedures before the fertilization process can even begin to be attempted. In vitro has only a 15-30 per cent success rate and costs between eight and fifteen thousand dollars. Many couples have been able to conceive children who otherwise couldn't without the help of these medical methods. When in vitro works, it is wonderful. When it doesn't, the emotional, physical, and financial toll on a couple is very steep indeed.

After two years of undergoing various treatments, Cherise and Theodore lost their first children right before Christmas. It was a sad season for them but their hopes rose in the new year as they decided to try the process again armed with some new information and more probable procedures. During this time, Theodore was able to tell Cherise about his discomfort with the idea of adoption. They had begun to take some steps toward adoption before Theodore led them onto the in vitro road. Raised in a home darkened by prejudice, he was not only worried his parents would not accept adopted children, he was also not sure he himself could. He felt he couldn't, and shouldn't, adopt.

Cherise had to face the fact that they were almost out of options. If this round of in vitro wasn't successful, they would have to remain childless. Within the next few months they would know whether or not there would ever be children in their family. Cherise hoped for the best, but began to prepare herself to accept the death of her dream. She knew she may very well need to find the strength to let go of her deep desire to become a mother.

There is an innate, intense longing for children that women experience, which men do not seem to experience nearly as deeply. Through the people I have met, and the reading I have done, I have come to notice that it is generally the women who are the initiators in a couple's decision to conceive or adopt a child. Once the child arrives, the father is often proud and thrilled, but it is almost always the mother who is the catalyst for the coming of the child.

Typically, while a man is sensitive to his wife's desire to have a child, he is often largely immune to the effects of this all-consuming ache. He may even feel hurt by it, wondering why his wife isn't satisfied with just him. The questions Hannah's husband asked her thousands of years ago reflect the male ignorance of the maternal yearning: "Why are you downhearted? Don't I mean more to you than ten sons?"[2] Theodore was significantly more sensitive than Hannah's husband. One night, while watching TV, he heard a character state that someone was like a mother without a child. He remarked thoughtfully to Cherise, "That's like you."

Theodore was happy with his life with Cherise and didn't feel he needed anything or anyone else. Cherise was also happy with her life with Theodore, and wanted children to celebrate and cement their relationship. When it became apparent there was a strong possibility that they would not become parents, she began to let go of her hopes. Since Theodore is an easy-going sort of person, she knew he would agree to an adoption if she begged or pushed, but she set aside her own feelings in favor of her husband's, demonstrating a deep faithfulness both to him and to his family. Where many women would have been racked with resentment and self-pity, Cherise stubbornly chose love and acceptance. As deep as her longings ran for children, she did not want anything to come between her and the man she pledged her life to.

Cherise made plans to change professions from daycare work to seniors work, knowing that such close contact with young children would be too painful to continue on a daily basis. She headed courageously into a second round of hormones, needles, and painful personal procedures. The sailing wasn't smooth. It seemed there were constant crises to get through. Would she come out of surgery with everything intact? Would her hormone levels drop enough to be able to continue the process?

Her doctor's office was somewhat near my house and she stopped by to visit sometimes between her frequent appointments, bringing candy and telling stories of the skunks that were roaming her neighborhood; while inwardly wrestling with worry over the current crisis. By the end of the seemingly endless process things were falling into place perfectly, and things were looking good. I was almost positive the procedures would work out positively, even after Cherise became very ill and developed a high fever.

"It wasn't meant to be," Cherise's gentle voice said when she called to tell me it was all over. Blood tests had confirmed that she had lost the babies. How could this be? How could they go on? How could they get over this? "God has a plan. I just don't know what it is yet," she said softly but firmly, knowing full well she was out of options. Cherise is a powerful model of unconditional faithfulness to me.

I brought some soup over to her house the night after they got the devastating news. I was prepared to comfort; to listen to anger, doubt, and despair with compassion and without platitudes. But there was no anger, no doubt, and no despair to listen to. She showed me all the things she loved in her yard, talked about fishing, baked some apple crisp, and told me about the new job she had started that day. She was not burying her grief. She was continuing on with life in spite of it. She was not ignoring her loss. She had pre-accepted it and was already moving on and up.

As I watched Cherise suffer through the "procedures" involving surgery, daily needles, daily doctor visits, weight gain, headaches, insomnia, emotional challenges, physical pain, bleeding, nausea and vomiting, I made some inner vows: If I get pregnant, I will not complain or indulge in self-pity about how I feel and what I'm suffering. Instead of comparing my situation with women who don't suffer much during pregnancy, I will remember Cherise and the things she's suffered, sacrificed and lost.

After Cherise lost her last babies, my heart would ache for her whenever I felt the softness of a little hand in mine, or saw a small head cuddled against a mother's breast. I felt angry with people who did not seem to appreciate their children, and people who flaunted their fertility, or took it for granted. I wondered why Cherise and Theodore couldn't be given children, why it had looked like God was leading them to undergo in vitro, and why abusive, neglectful people got to be parents and they didn't.

I was amazed to see Cherise, though I probably shouldn't have been, at a baby shower shortly after she had lost her last babies. She had bought extra little gifts for one baby's older siblings out of the money she and Theodore had left after their expensive procedures. From my position behind the dessert table I watched Cherise cradling one of the new babies. If this was hard for me, what must it have been like for her? I found myself pleading a bottomless, seemingly senseless, heart-cry: *Oh Lord, fill her arms.*

CHAPTER TWO

A Sad Ending

After about a year and a half of trying to conceive something strange happened. I began to bleed at a time when I shouldn't have been bleeding at all. Pink blood, a new concept for me, turned into fragments of brown blood before increasing to quite a lot of regular red blood that would start and stop quite erratically. I was quite confused about the whole matter and probably started to think about things like cancer. Herb was out of town for work and I didn't know what I would do with Tim if something went seriously wrong. Since I didn't know what was going on let alone what might still happen I wasn't sure whether I should just keep on with my plans or try to get in to see my doctor. One night I bled pretty hard and just prayed I wouldn't fall right apart before Herb got home.

When I did get to a doctor, not my regular one, he too was confused about what could be happening. He said my right ovary was swollen, probably due to ovulation, but he asked himself out loud, "Why is the bleeding happening?" He ordered a pregnancy test, which I thought was particularly idiotic since it was clear I could not be pregnant. The next morning, still bleeding, I got in to see my regular doctor. After waiting for far too long with two-year-old Timmy I was called into the office and received a serious shock as I walked in the door and caught a glimpse of a yellow post-it note on the outside of my file: "Liz Adam – pregnancy positive." *How could this be?* My mind raced and my legs shook as I read Timmy some sort of ancient doctor's office book.

When the doctor whooshed in he informed me I was in the process of losing a baby. According to him, it was for the best because some medication I'd had to take recently for an infection wasn't safe for pregnancy. He gave me a pat on the shoulder and walked out of the room. I wanted to burst into tears but didn't. "Can't you do anything?" I might have asked if I hadn't been so shocked, but I went home quietly and cried on Herb's lap. As if the double-fronted news of being pregnant and losing the baby were not enough for one day, that very same day we had to look at and make an offer on a house. I did not sleep much that night.

The bleeding went on for another whole week, vacillating between severe and light. I silently willed the baby to hang in there, especially after I found out my HCG levels were rising instead of dropping. I loved this child the moment I found out there was one but I think I knew deep down that something was not right, despite my efforts to convince myself otherwise. I went to the library, took out a stack of pregnancy books, and read them late into the night, worrying and wondering what I should do next.

By morning, the answer was clear. I needed to go to emergency. Herb brought me there while it was still dark with a frightened little Timmy still dressed in his red fuzzy pajamas. We were the only people in the waiting room, not counting the carpet cleaners, but I was parked underneath a white board in the hallway across from the nurses' station until mid-afternoon when I could get in for an ultrasound. As the seven hours ticked by in a less-than-peaceful environment, I yearned for the life inside of me to keep living. *Live, little one*, I silently and frequently urged, *Hang in there.*

The ultrasound hurt more than it should have. Exterior ultrasounds are one thing. Interior ultrasounds (with the wand in places you would rather not have a wand in) are quite another—especially if you are already bleeding and in pain. The technician kept getting annoyed about not being able to see something and tried to shove the wand in further. She told me nothing but I looked at the clipboard she laid on my legs after setting me aside for shipping: Right side – ectopic. The word ectopic was circled. I still hoped against hope. Maybe they could move it.

When I got back to emergency I was quickly prepared for surgery and told I might not have a tube when I woke up. I would have to have a full incision and stay in the hospital for two days afterward. And, no, the baby could not be moved. I had to sign consent forms, rather shakily due to shock and the rapidly-administered morphine that was beginning to kick in. I was deeply disturbed by the knowledge that we had a baby – it was just in the wrong spot, just an inch or two from where it could develop into a child to have and to hold. We were so close, and yet so helplessly far.

They let me call Herb. He and Timmy came to see me before I went in for surgery. Since I was pumped full of morphine as soon as I came back from the ultrasound, I don't remember much of this visit but I do remember how nice my nurse and the anesthetist were. And I can still see Herb's red jacket and worried expression. I told Herb and Timmy what was happening and must have made a strange face in an effort not to cry because Timmy remarked cheerfully, "That's a funny face." Then I did start to cry. Then Herb made a funny face.

Waking up from surgery, I was immediately told I still had a tube, which didn't seem like anything great at the time because the baby was gone. What bothered me most is that they took her out alive. Her tiny seven-week heart stopped beating when she was taken from me. The doctor told me he "milked it out of the tube" which I think was supposed to impress me, but only served to disturb me.

Herb and Tim came up to see me in the evenings after I was put in a hospital room for a couple of nights. They brought me a little brown stuffed puppy Timmy had picked out from a store. I thought this was a strange thing to bring a grown woman but it's become special over the years. We call it "hospital puppy" now because it's accompanied me to the hospital a number of times. I held it to my stomach that first night like it was the lost baby, and to my heart the second night like it was my little Timothy, who'd left the hospital crying because he'd had to leave me behind again.

The incision was huge and painful, a grisly smile from one side of my body to another. It hurt for months afterward. The day after I got home from the hospital my brother James and his new wife Carmela came over and made me laugh so hard I split a part of my incision open. Carmela told me she'd written "sarb" (bras written backwards) on their grocery list in an attempt to remind herself to buy bras without having James's friends see the word "bras" written on the fridge when they came over. The funny part is that when James went grocery shopping he spent a really long time looking for something called "sarb" and even broke a sacred male tradition by asking for help when he became completely baffled. The store clerk thought it might be some kind of fish, so they searched the frozen fish aisle together, all to no avail. This story cracked me up, literally.

My Mom came in to take care of Timmy since Herb had to go back to work. Now that I am thinking about it, I do not remember calling her. I guess Herb must have. I do remember her arriving. I was propped up in bed in a floral nightgown and wool socks, feeling very low. She came quietly into the room and sat on the edge of my bed. For some reason, I could not look at her. I could feel her looking at me with compassion but I did not lift my eyes to hers, staring instead at the wooden edge of the bed.

Mom has experienced worse and more of this same grief. She "lost" a number of babies between me and my brother, who is almost five years younger than I am. Some of these miscarriages were awful experiences–one was almost five months along. In her pictures during those years she looks pale and weak, no doubt from blood loss and sorrow. My Dad says he would wake up at night and hear her crying downstairs. Mom and I are alike this way. We grieve alone, for better or for worse.

I didn't really begin to feel the loss until almost two weeks after the surgery. Until that time I was in a state of numb shock. The grief struck at a bad time. Herb's brother was visiting from out of town, excited about showing off his new girlfriend. Herb could sense I was in a bad sort of state and took them out somewhere one morning while I lay on the couch and cried, my heart crushed with longing to hold a tiny hand.

We refer to this baby as a girl not because we had any physical proof of femaleness but because Herb had a feeling she was a girl. He thought we should name her Angela, which means "A little angel". I bought a glass angel Christmas tree ornament and tied a gold ribbon onto it, writing her name and the date she died in white letters: Baby Angela, October 30th, 1998.

An ectopic pregnancy is one of those things I just skipped over when I read pregnancy books, assuming it would never happen to me. But it did happen to me, and I am thankful to have lived through it. If I lived in another time period, or even another country, I almost certainly wouldn't have lived to tell this story as the baby would have continued to grow inside my tube undetected. Within a short period of time the tube would have ruptured and caused fatal internal bleeding.

I am glad I can still be here for everyone and everything God wants me to be here for. Every once in a while, Tim will talk about having a brother or sister in heaven, especially when he comes across the angel ornament as we decorate the Christmas tree every year. He seems to have an unspoken understanding that it is a very special ornament. He never hangs it on the tree even though he is allowed to hang any ornament he wants. He instinctively leaves it for me. I always place it so a light shines through the little angel. Though I have yet to see her, I know she's beautiful.

Dayna's Story

Dayna had a perfect pregnancy. After a few years of being married she and her husband Chris were thrilled to be expecting a baby, after about a year of trying to conceive. Since Dayna is anemic, the extra blood that pregnancy produced in her body caused her to feel healthier and more energetic than ever before. The happy couple bought a house to hold their growing family and were able to move into it and set up a baby's room about six weeks before their baby was due to arrive on November 5th.

The night before Halloween Dayna felt a strong, sudden gush at two o'clock in the morning while she was in bed and assumed her water must have broken. She felt her way down the dark hallway and into the bathroom. Chris heard her leave, came behind her, and turned on the light for her. That was when they saw the blood—everywhere. "It looked like someone had been murdered," Dayna said. The gush she had felt was not water, but blood, and there was a lot of it. All down the hallway from the bedroom to the bathroom, there was a trail of blood.

Chris called the doctor's emergency line. He was told to hang up and call 911 immediately. An ambulance came and rushed Dayna, still bleeding profusely, into the nearest hospital. She began to go into shock, shaking violently. One of Dayna's aunts happened to be the on-call nurse that night and Dayna can remember a voice saying to her, "It's Auntie Linda. Everything's going to be fine." Dayna was rushed to an operating room and put under general anaesthetic for an emergency C-section.

At about six in the morning Dayna came out of the anaesthetic. She saw Chris at the foot of the bed and asked him excitedly, "What is it? What is it?"

He turned to look at her and she saw his face drop dramatically. "It's a boy," he told her.

"I told you. I told you it was a boy," she said, elated.

Chris couldn't look at his wife. He walked out of the room.

After some time Baby Dillon was brought into Dayna's room. At ten pounds six ounces he was a huge baby even though he was a week early. Dillon was full of tubes, but Dayna still did not, could not, and would not put her head around the fact that something was very wrong.

The blood Dayna had lost was mostly Dillon's blood. Baby Dillon had been born with no brain activity. Hospital staff worked to revive Dillon for twenty-five minutes after his emergency Caesarean delivery and were just about to give up when his heart started beating. Doctors were amazed, but the baby's brain activity did not return. The heart services unit from another hospital came to get Dillon. Chris stood haltingly by the edge of Dayna's bed, torn between staying with his wife and going with his child. Dayna told him to go with their baby. She had no choice but to stay behind, holding only two Polaroid pictures of the baby she hadn't been able to hold yet.

Some time later Dayna was transported to the same hospital Dillon had been taken to. A nurse that had been with her all along went beyond the call of duty and went along with Dayna to the other hospital. When Dayna went into the Intensive Care Unit to see Dillon she could hardly believe he belonged there. All the other babies were so tiny that Dillon looked very large and out-of-place. Dayna had been telling herself all along, "He'll be fine." But when she saw Dillon in the ICU unit full of tubes with blood coming out of his nose, the insufferable, unbelievable truth was the hardest thing she's ever had to deal with. "At that point I knew something was really wrong."

Dillon was "living" only because he was hooked up to life support machines. Although his heart had by now stopped beating, and he never had never had any brain activity, the staff kept him on life support for several hours while Chris and Dayna tried to come to terms with everything that had happened. Doctors told them they needed to give permission for their baby to be taken off of life support. "I need to hold him," Dayna told them.

The family was taken to a family room. Dillon was taken off life support and brought to them. When Dayna took him in her arms she felt the air coming out of his body from the life support and exclaimed, "He's breathing! He's breathing!" But he wasn't. Dayna held Dillon for hours and couldn't let go of him. They took pictures. They had him baptized. After a long time, Dayna's father said, "I can't watch you do this anymore," and took Dillon away. After he was gone, Dayna began to scream uncontrollably. A nurse told her they could bring the baby back if she wanted. But that's not what she wanted.

Dayna had originally been brought to a floor of the hospital on which everyone had a baby. She was moved to another floor, on which no one had a baby. By this point Dayna had been in a wheelchair for eight torturous hours without any pain medication. Her mother-in-law had to fight to get the staff to give Dayna something to lessen her pain, the part of her pain that could be lessened. "Is she asking for something already?" a nurse questioned. Back in her room, Dayna began to cry so hard that she began to hyperventilate. She couldn't sleep. Nurses brought her sleeping pills. She still couldn't sleep. She needed answers. What had happened? Nobody could give her any of the answers she needed.

The family cleaned the carpets and packed away all the baby's things. Chris and Dayna came home to a house that felt far too empty. Dayna also felt extremely empty inside. Sometimes when she first woke she would feel like she was still pregnant. As she became more conscious, she would remember her emptiness and be filled with almost unbearable sorrow. On her first day at home after being released from the hospital, Dayna was by herself and just couldn't cope with the grief on her own. She called Chris several times at work, who realized she needed more support and arranged for Dayna's mother to come and stay with her.

Chris's grief and anger over his baby's death got unleashed at their doctor when they went in for Dayna's post-partum check-up. Chris asked to speak to the doctor alone. Through the office walls, Dayna could hear him yelling at the doctor, and the doctor telling him there was nothing she could have done. When something unexplainably horrible happens, people seem to need someone or something to blame. Dayna wondered if the ultrasound technician could have missed seeing the cause of Dillon's death that was finally identified. One of the blood vessels of the umbilical cord had detached from the rest of the cord and was lying along the opening to Dayna's cervix. As soon as the cervix began to dilate in labor, the blood vessel ruptured, and Dillon lost his blood supply.

Whether or not a medical mistake was made Dillon was gone, and there was nothing Chris or Dayna or any doctor could do to bring him back. They had him cremated and had a service for him, rather than participating in the mass cremation and memorial service the hospital performs on a regular basis for infants who have died over a period of time. Then they placed Dillon's ashes and his pictures up on a special shelf in their home.

The months following Dillon's death were bleak and lonely. The sad couple went through the Christmas season without the baby they had expected would be bringing them much joy on his or her first Christmas. Then came the many long, dark, lonely days of a Winnipeg winter. Dayna took six months off from her job as a hairstylist. She needed time for customers to hear about her loss from someone other than her. She couldn't face having to tell her clients what had happened over and over again when they would undoubtedly ask about her new baby. Dayna went back to work in April. In August she found out she was pregnant again.

Dayna had another perfect pregnancy, except this time she felt very anxious, and worried all the way through her pregnancy, which was carefully monitored with ultrasounds and fetal assessments. Her doctor planned a pre-scheduled caesarean delivery for almost a month before the baby was due. The day before the scheduled delivery Dayna had to undergo an amniocentesis analysis to test the baby's lung development. The test was awful for Dayna and upset her terribly because she had to sign papers specifying some very severe risks of the procedure. The test indicated that the baby's lungs weren't ready yet and the scheduled delivery was put off, first for one week, then another. Dayna became very fearful as the days went by, and became convinced that this baby was going to die too.

When the baby's lungs were finally deemed ready, a Caesarean was performed, with Dayna awake this time. The baby came out screaming–and Dayna said it was the best sound she had ever heard. A year and a half after watching her first baby die, she got to hear and see her second baby live–a healthy baby girl. "She could scream forever," Dayna said.

Baby Mikayla had some fluid on her lungs and needed a chest x-ray and an IV line. Seeing her daughter lying in a bed identical to the one her son had lain in was disconcerting, but different because

Mikayla's eyes were open and her arms were moving. Today, Mikayla is a beautiful little girl with sparkly blue eyes and chubby cheeks. She is a delight to her parents and everyone around her.

Someone who didn't really understand might say this story has a happy ending. And in a way, it certainly does if one considers several other endings it could have had. But in another way, it doesn't. While it is wonderful that Chris and Dayna have another child to love and care for, it does not change the fact that they have lost a child. Even though Chris and Dayna have been able to begin a bright new chapter in their story, they have not tried to shred the sad part by dismissing or forgetting about Dillon. They have kept moving forward, but nothing will ever take the memories of their first child out of their hearts. They will think of him often, and the love they have for him will remain until they can see him again, joyful and whole.

Another reason why this story doesn't really have a happy ending is because it hasn't ended. It is just beginning. Within the little pink-bibbed baby snuggling into her Mommy's lap are a lifetime of experiences yet to unfold— events waiting to happen, personality beginning to bud, interests about to appear, gifts waiting to be unwrapped. Will she like school? Who will she love? What sorts of work will she do? Will she have her own children to snuggle on her lap?

Dayna's motherhood story is just beginning. The pages will turn rapidly, recording all different sorts of experiences and emotions. At the end, everything really will be fine, for the darkest of sorrows will become the brightest of joys.

On Family and Forever

Families seem to enjoy trying to figure out family likenesses, especially right after a baby is born, which is really quite silly considering how babies generally look right after they're born ("Let's see, who is it that has a cone-shaped head and squished eyes? That must be from the other side."). While family resemblances can be meaningful, children are more than just some combination of miscellaneous relatives. They are completely unique creations, and I firmly believe that children who come into a family either by birth or by adoption come there by design. People are placed together on purpose and whether or not those purposes are fulfilled, the power of relationship remains—for better or for worse.

So here Herb and I are, already immortalized as Mom and Dad. May we bear these roles with the honor they deserve. Sometimes, holding the title and position of Mommy has felt like pretending, like I am too young to actually be a mother. At other times, being the Mom has felt very obvious and natural. Sometimes I feel like I'm doing a great job as a mother—other times I feel like I am seriously scarring my children. Sometimes I wonder…How do my children see me? What will they think about my mothering when they are older? What will they say? What sorts of memories will they have?

Anna Quindlen notices, "Our mothers only slowly become people to us, as we grow older and they do, too..."[1] I believe that same statement holds true for the other people we've grown up with. Only as we mature, or perhaps I should say only *if* we mature, do we begin to think and care about exactly who our family members are, how they feel, and what they think. While it is not completely uncommon for people to remain self-centered all their lives, we hopefully come to see and embrace the fact that our mothers, fathers, brothers, sisters, husbands, and children have personalities, dreams, minds, and feelings of their own. Their lives do not and should not center around ours. When we start to see this, the people around us become people to us.

My mother is a very sensitive person. She picks up on things that most people would never even think about noticing. She is compassionate, gracious, and very shy by nature. She doesn't set her foot down very often but when she sets it down, it stays down. Mom taught in a one-room country school for seven years before I was born. She was a very caring teacher who went far beyond the call of duty. She was also quite strict and ran rather a tight ship, managing students who were bigger and often not much older than she was. Mom sometimes worked as a substitute teacher during our growing-up years. One of our favorite stories is Mom sweeping an unruly student out of the classroom with a broom from the coat closet, since a strap was no longer at her disposal.

As a mother, Mom did lay down the law when she needed to, like when my brother James was hammering the piano keys with an actual hammer, but she let her gentle nature prevail more since she wasn't as outnumbered in the home as in the classroom. She was and still is a very dedicated and caring mother. I was writing on my parent's computer a couple of weeks ago and came across a file I had forgotten about. Several years ago I'd asked a number of experienced mothers, including my own mother, what advice they would give to newer mothers. Reading through the advice Mom wrote I noticed how she's practiced everything she preached: "Enjoy your children", "Be a peacemaker", "Encourage and praise your little one", "Raise them to be independent from you and dependent on God"; and then I smiled as I read her last piece of advice: "Visit Grama and Grampa often." Mom has a quietly funny sense of humor and is very selfless and compassionate. She is also a woman of immense emotional fortitude. She has persevered and is continuing to persevere through a number of difficult circumstances with almost incredible grace.

My parents met as children in school after my Dad's Austrian family immigrated to our small town when Dad was thirteen. He finished grade eight before he went to work as a mechanic in order to earn money to help support the struggling family. Never having enjoyed school much anyway, it wasn't long before he began to pursue his own ventures including a number of vehicle-based businesses, a logging company, and a cattle farm.

My parents are a case study for the saying "opposites attract". Over their years together, they have become more and more alike, meeting in the middle of their rather extreme personalities, while somehow managing to maintain their own identities. If opposites naturally attract, there must be purposes behind those attractions– to unite, to strengthen, to complete, and to create. Now that I can see my parents' merger as the power source it was intended to be I am asking God to give me my father's passion and my mother's patience; my father's drive and my mother's discernment; my father's vision, my mother's compassion, my father's courage, and my mother's grace. I know I am asking for a lot, but I also know there are no limits to these sorts of things. God possesses and produces things like grace and passion in infinite amounts and He is just waiting to give some to anyone who'll receive.

My Dad is the sort of person who is almost impossible to describe in a paragraph or two, partly because he has been changing at rather rapid rates in recent years. Not long ago my parents made the wise decision to sell their forty-year-old car dealership. When I was looking through a retirement scrapbook that my sister-in-law Carmela put together for them I was sort of surprised to see that many of the mechanics had thanked Dad for being patient with them, which is not a word I would have used to describe Dad in earlier years. He has changed by degrees into a man whose character is as strong as his personality.

Largely unaware of the immense amount of respect he has garnered throughout his family and community, Dad still seems to see himself as insecure, as though he hasn't realized that he has turned from a caboose into an engine. In spite of his self-diagnosed "graphic dyslexia", "displaced person syndrome", and grade eight education that he brings up on a regular basis, Dad has developed an immense realm of skills including operating bulldozers, deciphering engineering reports, and cleaning partridges with his bare hands. The things he can't do, like tell jokes and operate bank machines, provide plenty of material for my brother's hilarious sense of humor.

We came very close to losing my Dad a few years ago when a major blood vessel burst in his brain one night while he was out baling hay. He drove himself home in the tractor, barely getting himself inside the house where my Mom took one look at him, called an ambulance and eventually got him airlifted into Winnipeg, insisting on accompanying him in the air ambulance. (This was one of the times she set her foot down.) When I first saw Dad in emergency he said, "This would be a good time to pray for me." I did, laying my hand on his heart. I told him God's mercy is very great and he said, "He's not going to get me yet. I still have to see my grandson." Nobody on earth knew that the baby I was carrying was a boy. I wonder, was he close enough to heaven to see who was on the way to earth? I guess he couldn't have been too close or he wouldn't feel like God was out to "get" him.

Dad came out of surgery the next morning quite spry but quickly plunged into one serious danger after another. Several times it looked like he might not live. He lay hooked up to multitudes of beeping machines in intensive care and we sat beside him, wondering if he was going to live or not. It was a surreal sort of experience to see my indomitable father lying flat in bed in a hospital gown that did not fit him at all, and downright agonizing to watch him try to communicate with breathing and stomach tubes down his throat. As I sat beside his bed one late night in intensive care he pointed to himself and then up to the sky. I wondered if he was trying to tell me he was going to heaven.

As soon as Dad realized he was going to live he told the intensive care staff he was through with them and was going to leave. One nurse knew how to deal with his type and made him stand up and prove to her that he could walk. When he realized he couldn't, he stayed put awhile longer—five horribly long weeks altogether. They let him go home for a long weekend and he horrified Mom by driving into town when she slipped out for a couple of minutes to get groceries. Although his license had been taken away after the aneurysm, she shouldn't have been shocked. After all, my brother James had accidentally run into Dad's leg with a truck a few years previous and Dad still drove even with a full cast on his left leg—he just sat over on the passenger's side and reached over toward the steering wheel, which provided rather a startling sight for the people he met on the road. The powers that be at the hospital didn't want to let Dad go because he was doing things like crossing the road against red lights when they would take him out for assessments. We knew this was a sign he was back to his regular self.

Dad has grown significantly stronger in the last number of years. It is a strength born of weakness, of the loss and the giving up of control, of a brush with mortality, of the wisdom of experience, and of lessons learned. He has changed both in big ways and in small ones. One sometimes-amusing change is his recent attempts at doing some things around the house. In theory, a Class A mechanic would be able to operate a vacuum cleaner without much difficulty, but men's work skills don't seem to transfer home sometimes.

For many people, the concept of a man making breakfast for himself is not revolutionary. For those with some exposure to certain types of men, you realize how groundbreaking this can be. I am talking about a man who took it into his head to be extra-independent one evening by toasting himself a bun for supper. He did so by turning the stove element on high, setting a bun on it, and going in to watch TV. On my last visit, Mom had recently torn a ligament in her leg climbing into one of Dad's logging trucks and Dad made himself breakfast every morning—eggs and bratwurst made from one of our own cows. I offered to do it for him but he told me, "No. I'm a survivor", and proceeded to fix his breakfast with great intensity.

"I've come a long ways," he announced after a few minutes of very focused frying, waving his masterpiece under my nose.

"You have," I said.

We all have.

Herb has three younger brothers—Ed, Bernie, and Marc. The four boys were born in six years. Though I was not around when they were growing up, I am thinking it was probably a pretty busy household. On one occasion a neighbor phoned Herb's Mom to tell her that the boys were on the roof. "I know," she said. She was probably happy to have them out of the house for a bit. I have heard reports of their hide-and-seek games, which involved turning off the lights in the basement, perching on a rafter, and pouncing on whoever was "it" when they walked underneath.

I have one younger brother, James, who still doesn't know how to find "sarb" in a grocery store despite becoming a father in intervening years. He has always been an entertaining person to be around with a character all his own. He is working with Dad in the timber business now, which can also be entertaining, at least for me. I laughed when I saw a post-it note in James's handwriting up on Dad's computer monitor with step-by-step instructions on how to check something or other. It started with "Step 1: Turn on computer." James is caring, smart, funny, and gifted in a number of different areas.

All of our brothers are married now—much to my mother-in-law's relief. All have married well. I went from being the only girl around to having four sisters-in-law within a few years and now a good crop of cousins has sprung up rather rapidly. Herb and I have only one remaining grandparent between the two of us—my Dad's Austrian mother who we call "Oma". She is currently ninety-two years old and has moved off the farm my Dad's family originally immigrated to and into a seniors' apartment in town after a series of dangerous driving escapades and a health scare.

I have a friend who is a social worker for an adoption agency. She likes working with adoptive families because "they don't expect everything to be perfect." This realistic expectation is something I am learning, slowly but surely. Since I have had both perfectionistic and critical tendencies, it's easy for me to get upset over something that's gone wrong instead of enjoying all the things that haven't. I am learning how to focus on the good things about people and situations instead of the not-so-good. "Nobody's perfect" is a phrase

I've heard since childhood but haven't really absorbed and accepted until recently.

"A forever family" is a phrase that is fairly new to me. Until I heard it, I had never consciously thought about the fact that a family is for always, for better or for worse. A family is a "till death do us part" sort of thing and even when death does part, a certain unity of spirit remains. Deaths, divorces, moves, marriages, feuds, and additions happen, but the power of family remains strong in each individual, and in the family as a whole. As mighty as mother love is, it is one strength among many that can be in operation within a family—and empowering every one is the divine love that creates, sustains, and reigns over all.

Lisa's Story

Generally, interviews I conduct are rather relaxed sorts of affairs. This one is particularly so. Lisa and I are both wearing old sweat pants, having decided not to meet in a restaurant since both of us know we will probably both cry. I have a Kleenex box within arm's reach and a blue vinyl clipboard beside me on which I occasionally scratch notes. Lisa is lying on the couch with her feet up on the back of it. I am hanging out on a big pillow on the floor, smelling strongly of A5-35. Our children have been left with their respective fathers for bedtime, which we stretch well past midnight even though Lisa has to be up at five to get ready to go to work.

Whenever I interview someone I always learn something new, even if the person is a good friend of mine. Often, I think I know about someone's experiences, thoughts, or feelings but find myself surprised over something or other, and glad for the opportunity to learn deeper things about people that I probably wouldn't have otherwise.

Lisa has changed rather remarkably since the first time I met her about ten years ago. Her nose ring is gone, for example. She's stopped smoking. She's started smiling a lot more. And there have been some very significant internal renovations going on, less obvious to an outside observer but far more transformational than any exterior change. Lisa and her husband Rod both look so different from the way they used to look that their son stared at their engagement picture one day and asked, "Who are those people?"

Rod and Lisa were married when Lisa was just twenty. She was old for her age though, having already lived through maternal abuse and several sorts of substance abuse. She'd left home at eighteen and lived with a friend for a year and then with Rod for over a year before getting married. Lisa wanted to have a child as soon as they were married.

"I didn't really know what a mother was supposed to be," she says to me, "I knew I would be a good mother, but I didn't have anything to base it on. I had to venture into being a mother with no modeling whatsoever."

Lisa was adopted as a newborn in 1967 after her adoptive mother suffered several miscarriages and a death in the family, partly because a psychiatrist had advised that adopting a baby would make her mother feel better. Lisa's mother was horribly abused by her own father as a child, and suffered from mental illness. As a result, she was unable to properly parent Lisa and Lisa's older brother. For the first years of Lisa's life her mother was emotionally absent, then for six or seven years she was physically abusive. After Lisa became big enough to fight back in her early teen years, her mother again became withdrawn and catatonic. Amazingly, Lisa feels she was damaged more by her mother's absence than by her abuse—a strong statement on the power of a mother's presence in a child's life.

Lisa had a good relationship with her father, who was the rock in her life, but she desperately needed women to care for her during the tumultuous teen years. She needed someone to talk to, and had to turn to the older girls in her church's youth group. Unfortunately, instead of being the role models and companions she needed, her peer group at church was an extremely negative influence. The older girls in the group pulled Lisa into drinking when she was just sixteen. After that, it wasn't long before she began experimenting with drugs with her friends from school. "Parents are ignorant when they want to be," Lisa states emphatically. Pretty well the entire youth group would come to church with hangovers and try to nurse their throbbing headaches in the back pew. "The light from the cross was blinding," she recalls.

When Lisa was seventeen, her father gave her a choice about whether or not to come to church. She came sporadically before making a complete break when she was getting ready to marry Rod. The pastor at the time refused to marry them since Rod wasn't a Christian, and didn't seem to want to meet with him. This drew the line for Lisa. "I hate your church," she told her father over the phone, "I hate those people."

Shortly after Rod and Lisa were married Lisa was diagnosed with polycystic ovarian syndrome. PCOS is a complex hormone disorder that usually begins to show itself at puberty with symptoms including weight gain, acne, dark body hair, skin flaps, migraines, depression, infertility and, obviously, ovarian cysts, which tend to grow and burst. Because there is a connection with insulin production, women with PCOS are also at increased risk for diabetes and heart disease. For six years Lisa did everything she could to help her body get pregnant. After diets, surgeries, and many rounds of drugs, the doctor told her it was time to give up. Devastated and angry, Lisa decided she'd start drinking again—but found she couldn't stand the taste of alcohol. She was pregnant.

Lisa became very ill during her pregnancy but was able to carry and deliver a healthy baby boy. After having Michael, Lisa found herself in post-partum depression. She sought help at a women's clinic, where counselors told her the depression was related to not receiving the love she had needed from her mother–but there was nothing that could really be done to fix the past. So Lisa went on with her life the best she could for a few years until she came to a point where it seemed like everything was on the rocks—her marriage, her work, her emotions, and her mothering.

After thirteen years of struggling, Lisa came to the point of extreme desperation she'd been heading toward for several years. She was desperate for meaning, for hope, and for love. Deep down, she knew where to find it. As soon as she stopped trying to run away from God, she began to stop hurting. Lisa found herself walking back into the church she felt had so failed and rejected her. As soon as she walked through the doors, she felt the church was significantly different than it had been before. "It's just a building," Rod told her after she told him what she'd felt. But something had changed and Lisa was drawn back, bringing both Rod and little Michael with her.

Michael is no longer little now but has grown rather rapidly into a junior higher. When he was almost ten years old, he got some surprising news from his parents. "It's funny," Lisa remarked, "The first thing Michael said when we told him we were going to have a baby was, 'Does this mean I'm not going to be an only child anymore?' I didn't think it was something he thought about." That remark reminded me of an icebreaker game we had played at church a few years ago which involved going around the room to find people with certain characteristics. One of the categories was "Is an only child" and Michael turned out to be the sole candidate in the room. Everybody clapped for Michael. After Tim found out there was going to be a baby in Michael's family he commented, "That's good. Me and Michael were getting tired of being only children." That comment surprised me, since we'd never really talked about him being an only child. Both Michael and Tim are getting past the age when a mother knows pretty well all their thoughts, and can predict with great accuracy what they're going to think or say about something.

The day Rod and Lisa announced they were going to be having a baby there was a general air of surprise and excitement. Since Lisa had told me about her disease, infertility, and how miraculous Michael's conception was, I knew that even though her heart hoped for another child, her mind realized it probably wouldn't be possible. I also knew Rod and Lisa were close to recommencing the adoption process they had begun and almost completed before Lisa got pregnant with Michael. What I did not know was that they had decided to give getting pregnant one last try. Lisa had gone to see her specialist and had been told she had a huge dermoid cyst that would have to be removed before she could even think about getting pregnant. Against all odds, she became pregnant during the months that she was waiting for surgery.

Two days after announcing her pregnancy, Lisa called me, crying. She had started to bleed. This miracle that she had thought was too good to be true wasn't going to come true. As she talked, weeping, I could hear her trying to make herself not care, almost mad at herself for caring so much, but deeply broken-hearted over losing her baby. That phone call opened my eyes to something I hadn't had the chance to see before—Lisa's mother-heart. I got the glimpse I needed to notice the tenderness and passion inside Lisa.

Lisa was convinced that it was all over. I listened to her and then began to pray that the bleeding would stop and the baby would live. The next morning as I watched the morning sun rise I had a sense, for the first time in my life, that a prayer mission was accomplished and all would be well. The bleeding stopped. The pregnancy continued, though not without further cause for concern. Several weeks after that scare my heart sank when Rod came to me at a church camp a few weeks later and told me Lisa wanted to see me. She was in her room lying down, bleeding and crying again. Again we hoped and prayed. Again the pregnancy survived.

Between her fourth and fifth month, Lisa began to bleed again and developed very severe pain. She went into emergency and was kept in the hospital for several days as doctors tried to manage her still-present cyst which had grown and twisted over a fallopian tube, causing intense pain. It was not until after this experience was over that Lisa began to take the guards off her heart and let herself care about the child she was carrying. At work one day a thought dropped into her head from above reminding her, "This is what you wanted." Lisa said she was glad she wasn't driving at the time because she was so taken aback that she might have had an accident.

After that very direct reminder, Lisa remembered a moment she'd somehow forgotten about. When a woman is suffering from infertility, she often feels a chronic, constant sadness deep inside that sometimes spikes into intense pain in certain conditions. Lisa had a strong spike of heartache while watching a Christmas performance of Handel's Messiah and seeing Mary holding Baby Jesus. She began to cry uncontrollably with anguish and anger over the news she'd recently received from her specialist about the cyst and over the fact that it was very unlikely she could have another baby at her age with her condition. God heard her cry, and by the next Christmas, Lisa held a new baby in her arms.

I went to the hospital to see Baby Jillian when she was born, or rather when she was cut out, in November. It was not an easy operation, recovery, or pregnancy for Lisa. She was less sick than she was with Michael, but had to deal with gestational diabetes and several other discomforts topped off with an unwanted Caesarean. When I got onto the high-risk floor of the hospital to see her we had a great visit, or so I thought. Lisa doesn't remember any of it due to the drugs she was on. I told her she sounded perfectly normal to me, and she told me it was just because she got so good at taking drugs and acting normal during her younger years.

After Jillian was born, Lisa and her Dad had a long talk about her adoption and childhood. Her Dad apologized for the way things were, and weren't. Lisa apologized for the trouble she caused. She is coming to fully realize and accept the fact that her mother didn't care for her because she couldn't care for her. Her adoptive mother was and still is mentally ill. Lisa still struggles with negative thoughts and emotions at times, but she is gaining ground rapidly. As she tells it she was "itching for a war" when she was pregnant with Jillian and was constantly picking fights with Rod. "I don't know how I got Rod," she's told me, "I wasn't doing anything to deserve him. He's got so much patience. I'm just so glad he puts up with me and my psychotic behavior."

Once when Lisa was quite pregnant we were sitting together on the edge of a sandbox, watching over a bunch of kids, and got talking about mother issues. Pregnancy was bringing her back to a place of grief and anger at her adoptive mother. "I got gypped," she stated, then looked down into the sand and started to talk about work. After her talk with her Dad, she was able to begin to let go of her deep-rooted maternal resentments. She has also received healing through connecting with her birthmother, Barb.

One of the most mind-boggling things that has ever happened to Lisa is hearing the phone ring one day when Michael was about four years old, and somehow knowing it was her birthmother calling. Lisa had registered at an agency a few months previous but had no other forewarning that her birthmother would be calling. Barb and Lisa talked for over three hours that night and met each other a few months later. Lisa was amazed at their similarities–they look alike, they think alike, they act alike, and they have similar tastes. During their first visit at Lisa's house they both decided to change into pajamas at the same time and came back wearing almost the same pajamas. As they shopped for baby clothes together one day, picking out the same sorts of things from opposite sides of the store, mother's and daughter's eyes met over a rack of clothes. Neither knew what to do with almost forty years worth of thoughts and feelings compressed into one chance glance.

Even though Lisa has a close relationship with her birthmother now, Lisa doesn't regret being adopted. She knows she needed to know the God her father introduced her to. She also enjoys being able to have an uncluttered adult relationship with Barb, free from the baggage she knows would be between them if Barb had raised her.

Lisa is letting herself love now, opening her heart to Jillian's chubby-cheeked smiles and Michael's wide-eyed gazes, letting herself rest in Rod's steady arms. She is a study in contrasts sometimes–feminine yet fierce, emotional but professional, guarded yet voluntarily vulnerable. Like most mothers, she can be both tough and tender, sometimes at the same time.

"My story's about someone who didn't have mother love but has God's love," Lisa concluded insightfully the night we talked for four and a half hours. It is God's protective love in her that roars to Michael's defense, His sacrificial love that watches over Jillian night and day through week-long infections, and His passionate love that cries at her baby's dedication service. Lisa now has free access to all the love she needs both for herself and her children. She knows where to find the ultimate love, the presence of which dispels the absence of any and all others.

Chapter 3

A Surprise Beginning

Was God trying to tell us something? After three years and three surgeries Herb and I began to wonder if maybe we were supposed to adopt instead of conceive a child. As we began to open our minds to this idea, our eyes were opened to the many children who so desperately need someone to love and care for them. What must it be like to be a child longing for a real family, fantasizing about the things that most children take for granted, as children should—parents to love them, a permanent home, food in the fridge, clothes and toys to call their own, brothers and sisters, grandparents, aunts, uncles, and cousins?

Our first major move toward adoption took place when my adoption worker friend happened to mention she was having trouble finding a home for a six-month-old baby boy. She said, half seriously, that she might have to take him home. I told Herb about this and he shocked me a few days later by saying he thought we should bring this baby into our family. I was not really ready for this, but the prospect of a baby is always exciting, especially after three years of trying to have one, and we ended up phoning our friend at home that night. She wisely told us that considering what we had just been through (I had just had my third surgery) it would not be a good time to make this decision or take on the responsibility of another child. Of course, she was right. But now the ball was rolling and picking up speed.

I began to think a lot about international adoption. We started making inquiries at different agencies and registered our names at our own government's agency. Somewhere along the line we must have started talking about international adoption with Timmy. I had no idea he was uneasy about it until my parents told me about a conversation they had with them when I wasn't around. He told them he was worried his Daddy and Mommy would go off to some faraway country for a baby and get killed there, or never come back. Up until that time I had known, or at least thought I knew, pretty well everything that went on in Timmy's mind.

We completed all the adoption classes just before Timmy turned five, jumping through hoops we didn't even have to think about before becoming Tim's parents. We filled out paperwork. We got references. We attended several seminars and an open house. Then we got referred to a very nice social worker and did three of the four visits required for her to complete a home study. We made plans to finish the fourth when we returned from a trip we were taking to Florida, ostensibly for a writers' conference held quite conveniently in the middle of a wicked Winnipeg winter. When our fourth home visit was complete, we would be approved by the agency and placed on the list of prospective adoptive parents. Then, we would just have to wait to be called.

Meanwhile, largely uninformed of our adoption journey, people were still praying for us to conceive a child. One friend found herself awake most of a night praying. Not coincidentally, that was the very month I got pregnant. Personally, I had pretty well quit praying, and almost quit hoping. People who don't know anything about infertility or prayer would say we conceived because of either taking a trip or getting close to adoption. We believe otherwise.

We do not know exactly what the end of our adoption story is. Even though this journey got re-routed, we believe it had a purpose. If nothing else, it has made us better people, and better parents. One of the questions we had to answer on our paperwork was, "Why do you want to be parents?"—a question everybody should have to think about before becoming parents. Is a parent's fulfillment the underlying goal of parenting? Our quest for a child also stretched our concepts of commitment—could we wholeheartedly embrace a child that many people around us would say is not "our own"? What is it that makes any child ours, anyway? Could we commit ourselves unconditionally to a child with behavioral problems, physical imperfections, or emotional difficulties?

I was extremely tired after coming home from our Florida trip. Part of this was due to the fact that I didn't sleep for an entire night after arriving home. Plus, I had a serious sleep deficit from the months leading up to the conference due to late-night computer work. And, unbeknownst to me, I was pregnant. I thought I was just short on sleep and long on PMS. When things dragged on I told myself not to think or care about it. I knew very well how heightened hopes have farther to fall. I had bled some pink blood that usually preceded my periods ever since the ectopic pregnancy. When nothing else followed after a few days I let myself do a test. I don't think any words I could use would accurately describe how I felt when I saw two lines appear on that test. Within seconds, that life-changing little line created a major mental switchover process, a whole new train of thought.

Herb was away on a work trip so I sat on the secret for a couple of days. Since it was right around Valentine's Day I gave him a pregnancy test wrapped in heart paper when he got home. Over the years, I have learned not to expect big reactions from Herb on things. I knew he wouldn't be whirling me around the room or anything. Men seem to need confirmation from a doctor, despite the fact that most doctors do exactly the same test mothers do at home. To be honest, I needed some more confirmation, too. After three surgeries and almost four years, the pregnancy felt unreal to me. It also took a number of weeks for me to mentally rule out the possibility of the baby being in the wrong place again. Things began to feel real the first time I threw up, twelve days after seeing the double lines. "Yep, I'm pregnant," I told myself as I lifted my head out of the toilet. It's funny how it all comes back. Back up, that is.

On the way home after a conference awhile ago, a lady sitting behind me on the airplane remarked dismally, "It's all coming back to me now," when the landscape rapidly changed from brown to white as we crossed what I will call a snow line. That is exactly how I felt after I started throwing up again. There is nothing like nausea to dim your outlook on life and while I was thrilled and thankful to be able to be pregnant again, I felt horrible both physically and emotionally. The days dragged as I suffered the basic equivalent of the stomach flu for seven weeks followed by another nine weeks of general grossness featuring almost incessant nausea and intermittent vomiting.

I had discovered near the end of my sickness with Timothy that slushies made with Coke or Pepsi (I know—not the healthiest sort of things for a developing baby) were about the only thing that helped alleviate nausea. People with severe nausea and vomiting learn that the traditional "crackers before rising" advice is a complete joke. All crackers do is scratch your throat when they come back up. Anyway, every morning Herb would head off to a convenience store and pick me up a slushie or two. He became rather a curious regular there, popping in at around six every morning in the dead of winter wearing his camouflage pants and red jacket. One morning the clerk couldn't help himself and inquired, "Breakfast?"

One of the many things I found challenging during my long stint of nausea and vomiting was Tim's fascination with frogs. We live near a park that has a little pond in it that is a literal breeding ground for wood frogs in spring. We have a springtime tradition of taking home some of the millions of eggs laid there, hatching them in containers on our deck, and making pets out of them for the summer, then putting them back before frost hits in September. While clumps of frog eggs are not generally good for nausea, it was the many gross and disturbing things frogs do when they are mating that really turned my stomach.

With all the natural education he was getting both at the frog pond and at my parents' farm, you would think Tim would have been able to draw some conclusions about how the baby got in my tummy, but he sort of asked the question a few times and I figured it was time to address it when he saw a stork in a picture and exclaimed, "Just what we need—a stork!" Upon my telling him that the stork was just a legend and didn't bring babies but rather God made them he said firmly, "But the stork put it in there, RIGHT?" I started to explain more accurately, but my explanations were arrested by Tim slamming his hands over his ears and yelling, "Stop talking!!!" I figured he wasn't quite ready for the technicalities yet, which was fine with me.

Tim's biggest concern about the whole affair seemed to be what we would name the baby. He started to make lists (by telling me what to write) of possible names—one sheet for a girl, and one for a boy. He would bring a pad of paper and come to "keep me company" in the living room where I was trying to gag down some food off a TV tray because I couldn't stand to sit at the dinner table. When we first told Tim we would be having a baby in our family he was thrilled and exclaimed, "FINALLY!" He woke Herb up that night at three in the morning to tell him, "Daddy! I thought of a name for the baby if it's a boy." When we would read books he would pick whatever name struck his fancy out of whatever story and hint as only little kids can hint, "Isabelle—that's a good name for a baby."

For me, the entire pregnancy was difficult in some way, which I didn't realize until two years after it was over though it seems rather obvious now. Immediately after I got over the months of being sick my Dad had his aneurysm and almost died. We were at the hospital almost every day for five weeks that felt like forever. After he was finally home and on the road to recuperation I was way too intensely trying to rewrite a manuscript before the baby came. I was also madly trying to do all the things around the house that so desperately needed to be done before the baby came and, of course, many which didn't really need to be done. I had insomnia, sciatic nerve problems, backache, low blood pressure, bleeding hemorrhoids, and was still nauseous sometimes. One lunchtime I was overtaxed by the frustrations I was having with my printer and with Tim's school bus driver and started to cry. Tim offered me the icing off his cake. Herb went to buy a new printer on his lunch break.

Even with my many discomforts, I wasn't wanting to get the pregnancy over with. I thought it would probably be my last one, and I did like feeling the baby moving around inside. Mostly though, I felt I had too much to do before the baby came and too little time to do it in. As my mother says, babies are easier to take care of inside than out. I walked very carefully and avoided anything that I thought might encourage labor. I knew my days were numbered and I was constantly counting days to estimate my amount of work time remaining. The only time I felt like it would be nice to be done being pregnant was when I had to get out of bed several times a night to go to the bathroom and felt so weak and tired doing so. However, I also knew I would still be getting up at night after the pregnancy was over, and the uptimes would be both longer and louder.

Every day when Timmy came home from kindergarten he would ask, "Did the baby break yet?" I made him a little baby advent calendar and he would religiously cross off a day as soon as he woke up in the morning. Kindergarten was kicking off with an in-depth study of colors. Each day was a different color theme and the kids were supposed to wear something of that particular color. Fittingly, on Red Day I started to bleed when I stepped out of the morning bath I took to ease the aches that had accumulated during the night. I was not expecting blood. I was ready for a burst of water again and this time I would know exactly what it was. I supposed this bit of blood must be connected to the ever-popular mucous plug all the books talk about. That night, four days before my due date, I started to get really uncomfortable in bed and went out into the living room to sit on the couch. The cradle in the living room was rocking back and forth all on its own, like a ticking clock. Then I realized my discomforts were actually contractions and they were getting pretty strong.

At 2:30 in the morning I called my Mom. She picked up the phone on the second ring and started the four-hour drive in to our city. At about 4:30 a.m. after many strong, regular contractions, I decided to lie down and try to get things to settle down until Mom arrived. The next thing I knew it was six and my labor seemed to have stopped. I bathed very carefully. Mom arrived when I was feeding Tim breakfast and settled in to stay awhile when it seemed that all contractions had completely evaporated. I did some sewing on a little blanket (I sew only when very pregnant, and not much then.) By afternoon, I decided to get things going by going for a brisk walk since I wasn't going to be able to get anything else done. After that brisk walk we went for another brisk walk.

Then things sped up very rapidly but I didn't tell anyone, including myself. I decided to wait until Herb had read Tim's bedtime story to him before heading to the hospital. Never in my life have I heard such a long chapter. I think I finally interrupted and convinced Herb it was definitely time to go. We took off as fast as I could waddle. We raced the midwife to the hospital and by the time I got up to the room I was in so much pain that I couldn't take my clothes off. Herb had to do it for me and get me up on the bed. "You're ten centimeters!" the midwife exclaimed when she checked me.

"I know," I told her. I wasn't surprised, just glad to be in the hospital instead of the van. In my desire to make sure I was actually in labor before I went to the hospital, I had waited too long. I arrived too late to receive the antibiotics I needed to counteract the Strep B infection I had. Two hours of IV are needed prior to birth to protect a baby from possible infection and death, but I landed up arriving only one hour before birth. I was stressed and felt out of control. The birth did not go at all the way I wanted it to. I wanted the pains to ease off just for a minute so I could regroup and catch my breath, but they didn't. They kept coming faster than I could manage them. Then the midwives told me the baby's heartbeat was dropping.

"It has to come out on the next push," the midwives kept telling me. This was easy for them to say. They were not lying flat on their backs facing an immovable mountain they had already been trying almost an hour to budge. Finally something came out, I will say the head, and then the baby stayed stuck there for what seemed like an eternity.

"Get it out," I begged the midwives.

"That's your job," they told me, not quite as sensitive as they could have been at the time. It eventually did come out, and it was a boy, purple and screaming. (Incidentally, it was Purple Day at kindergarten that day.)

It wasn't until six weeks after giving birth that I realized I didn't get to hold Daniel after he was born. I felt very upset when I realized this (since the awareness hit while listening to a conversation on the extreme importance of after-birth bonding) even though I knew the midwives were probably stressed about the cord being around the baby's neck and just didn't think of giving him to me after that was all looked after.

Instead of caressing the child I'd so stressfully delivered into the world, I lay on my back with my head turned way over, crotch throbbing, watching them bath and weigh the wailing baby I hadn't gotten to see yet. I wanted to comfort him but couldn't reach him.

Even from far off, I was surprised at how much dark hair Daniel had. Do all mothers expect their babies and births to be largely the same and get surprised when they aren't? After I finally got the chance to hold him and nurse him, it wasn't long before I began to worry about the baby's personality. He screamed a lot and wouldn't settle to sleep even after being nursed four times, and even though it was the middle of the night. Then somebody came in and said the baby's white blood cell count was abnormally high and he needed to be treated immediately. They took him away, and it felt like the floor dropped away from under my feet. I knew of a family who had lost their baby exactly this way, except in their case it was the staff's fault for not administering the IV. This was all my fault for not going to the hospital earlier. I was sick. Stunned. Scared.

The thought of losing this baby after everything we'd been through was both unbelievable and unbearable. Herb and I lay awake, speechless, in the dark hospital room on our separate beds, waiting for word. Would we really have to say good-bye to this baby so soon after saying hello? Would God really take him away? How could our family go on if this baby died?

I don't know how long it was before a pediatrician came into the room, her white coat glowing like an angel.

"Is his life in danger?" I asked her.

"Not at this point," she answered.

That was not the answer I was looking for. I asked her where he was, and if we could see him. They wheeled me down to the care unit and the sight of him alive comforted me, naked and startling under the bright lights, an IV line stuck into a tiny red foot. He was alive and moving. He was real. I reached out to touch him and started to cry. I wasn't allowed to hold him, just look at him. Then we had to leave him and go back to our room. They called our midwife and she came back to the hospital for us even though it was probably about four in the morning by this time. She came into our room to tell us not to worry. "He's in good hands," she told us. I think she meant the medical staff, but her statement had a deeper meaning to me.

By morning, Daniel's life was out of danger. I thank God. And may I never, never forget to be thankful for this child's life.

Becki's Story

Becki was born feet first just four minutes behind her twin brother. She weighed less than four pounds and had been inhaling amniotic fluid on her way out. Doctors worked on the tiny baby girl for an hour before they were able to tell her parents that she would be okay. Both babies stabilized quickly but had to remain at the hospital for some extra care after their mother was released. On one of Becki's father's visits to the hospital, a man shocked him by approaching him in the parking lot to ask if he could buy Becki to replace their family's baby that had died—an offer that was easy to refuse.

When the babies were big enough to be brought home, their mother, Carol, found caring for them to be a very demanding task. "I remember being so tired that I felt like throwing them out the window, but also knew that I would be there to catch them before they hit the ground," she wrote. Having narrowly escaped drowning at birth and not so narrowly escaped being sold or thrown out a window, Becki went on to have a happy childhood and youth, free from any complications of prematurity. When she was twenty-four she married Kelvin, a man she met through church and they began a new life together that involved plans to work together in full-time camp ministry. Kelvin had been working on a degree and they planned to start a family after he had finished school and found full-time work at a camp.

One day, a few months before their fourth anniversary, Becki began to suspect she may be pregnant. She waited until after Kelvin had left for school one morning, then took a pregnancy test. She was not at all thrilled to see a little plus sign appear. "Devastated," was the way she described her feelings. A baby was definitely not on her and Kelvin's agenda yet. They had just gotten to a point where they could begin to put away some money, and Becki had recently gotten a job she loved. "What is Kelvin going to say?" she wondered. Kelvin had recently decided to move into youth ministry instead of camp ministry, was working on finishing his degree again, and had already suffered some difficult setbacks.

Becki kept the life-changing news to herself for a week before she decided she couldn't go any longer without telling her husband. She told Kelvin she wanted to celebrate Valentine's Day a week early and gave him a present with two baby shirts tucked in the bottom. She had planned for them to read *I love my Mommy* and *I love my Daddy* but she has never gotten around to putting the decals on them.

"How did he react?" I asked Becki.

"Um…" she hesitated for quite a while, "He was surprised."

Becki had a camera ready to capture the look on Kelvin's face when he saw the shirts. "It looks like I missed the moment," she told me, "but I didn't."

After some time Kelvin came out of his state of shock enough to be able to pensively say, "Really!"

Neither Becki nor Kelvin felt emotionally or financially ready to have a child. For quite some time, their conversations revolved around asking each other, "What are we going to do?" and answering each other with, "I don't know." With Kelvin going back to school, they were having a hard time paying their rent and other expenses even though Becki was working two jobs. Fear and worry seemed to be the prominent emotions in their small apartment, but brief flashes of excitement would sometimes break through.

Becki experienced cramping early in the pregnancy, and for two or three weeks she silently hoped she would miscarry. "I never said it out loud. I don't even know if I ever told Kelvin." But then came a night when she was awake with very painful cramps in the middle of the night and found herself pleading *God, please don't take this baby.* That's when she realized her heart had come to love the child that her mind told her she didn't want yet.

For three months Becki suffered "morning" sickness that lessened but continued all throughout her pregnancy. She was working two jobs, one as our church's secretary and one at McDonald's. Perhaps there are worse jobs for a nauseous pregnant woman, like doing hospital laundry or slaughtering chickens or something, but I think McDonald's has to be one of the worst. The management was merciful enough to put her on drive-thru whenever possible. There were many days when Becki desperately wanted to call in sick but couldn't because they needed the money even more desperately.

At seventeen weeks gestation some standard screening tests were performed. Becki and Kelvin were apart for the weekend and when they saw each other again, Kelvin told Becki that the doctor's office had called and reported that the levels of the triple screening tests they had done came back abnormally high. The two shirts that Becki had given Kelvin for Valentine's Day turned out to be what some people might call foreshadowing. They were going to be having not one, but two unexpected babies.

On the bright side, Becki and Kelvin had significantly more time to prepare for twins than Becki's parents had. Becki and her brother were born in the 1970's, before ultrasound was available. Carol's doctor thought Carol was growing as if she was carrying twins, but could feel only one baby, and hear only one heartbeat. He kept asking her if there was any history of twins in her family, so the news wasn't a complete shock for Carol when it finally came. The doctor had been very hesitant to order an x-ray due to the potential danger to the developing baby, but eventually did arrange for one to confirm his suspicions. Six days later Carol delivered two babies.

Becki experienced the typical emotions common to most women when they find out they are going to become a mother—excitement, fear, nervousness, and very strange mixtures of all three, mingled with thoughts such as *Can I really do this?* and *Is this really going to happen?* Becki's thoughts and emotions were intensified by the element of surprise, and the challenges and changes unique to twins: Will it be a boy and a girl, two boys, or two girls? Can I handle them both? Becki comforted herself with the knowledge that God would not give her anything she couldn't handle.

At thirty-three weeks gestation, less than four months after Becki and Kelvin found out they would be having twins; Becki's membranes ruptured and she began leaking amniotic fluid. She was put on "active bed rest" and for two weeks continued on with life, feeling like a ticking time bomb and continually thirsty. One evening at home her water officially broke but when she went to the hospital she was sent back home because she wasn't having any contractions. On the way home from the hospital, however, she started having contractions. At one o'clock in the morning, water began gushing and they headed back to the hospital. Just before noon the next day their first baby, a boy they named Izak, was born. Between the births, the nurse suggested they take a family picture during the short space of time that they were a family of three. Becki thought it was a silly thing to think of at the time, but now she treasures that picture. As it turns out, they did have time for an intermission portrait session since labor stopped for some reason.

Becki needed to be induced to be able to deliver Aiden, one hour and twenty minutes after delivering Izak.

Becki's first three months with the babies are a haze for her. There were days she didn't get off the couch at all but spent the entire day nursing. Nights were short, long, and broken. People would often say off-handedly, "Oh, you're so lucky," thinking of the novelty of twins and how beautiful the babies were, but Becki sometimes felt frustrated at the flippant remarks. "People don't understand—it's a lot of work." Becki and Kelvin have also been the recipients of a number of outlandish comments and questions from strangers including, "They aren't twins. One has hair and one doesn't.", "How do you know they're twins?", or the socially difficult, "How did you conceive twins?"

Becki and Kelvin find it difficult to get any shopping or errands done with the two babies in tow. People keep stopping them to ask questions and make comments about the twins. They've learned to just keep on walking, letting people think they're rude—there's a limited amount of time in which to complete errands with two babies along. Sometimes trying to keep walking doesn't work for them because people will stop their cart right in front of the double stroller to look at the babies, preventing them from being able to get by. Sometimes each parent takes a baby to speed things up. Becki and Kelvin have developed a "divide and conquer" survival skill.

Like teammates, Becki and Kelvin work together well. Kelvin is rarely seen without a baby on an arm. "I want to say what a great dad I think Kelvin is," Becki came to tell me one Sunday after we'd talked about her story. "I wanted to add that in there." I smiled. She'd already told me that Kelvin is an amazing Dad, that she couldn't possibly imagine doing it without Kelvin, that the very thought of not having him scared her—but I was touched by her extra addition.

Quite some time after I began interviewing people for this book, I noticed that different women's stories seemed to sort of highlight different facets of mother love: perseverance, commitment, sacrifice, longing, passion, protection, transformation…As I listened to Becki chatter brightly about the provision of all the baby things they needed, how she worries about things like when to feed them strawberries, how she misses them when she's at work, how she spends money on them now instead of on herself, and how extremely serious and cute Izak was the first time he experienced an airplane's takeoff I wondered, "What is the theme here?"

Later, it came to me—acceptance. Becki has come to love and care for her children the same way she would if she had waited ten years for them. In the face of her initial devastation, she has accepted and welcomed these children with an open heart. Mother love has done its work in her. "There are no words for it," Becki said to me, unable to express how she feels when her heart feels full of love for her children. "The day Aiden learned to laugh, I laughed so hard I was crying."

This is what our children do to us. Opening our hearts to them fills us with a love that sometimes overflows inside of us, washing away all our devastations, our doubts, our fears, and our frustrations. I would be wrong if I made it sound like Becki, or any other mother in the world, has no hard feelings to deal with. I don't think I would be wrong if I said that every mother feels frustrated, impatient, angry, anxious, discouraged, or resentful sometimes. And I am quite sure I wouldn't be wrong if I stated that those sorts of feelings don't disprove our love. Every sort of feeling proves that we care enough about our children to be deeply affected by them.

On Anger and Forgiveness

My Mom once mentioned she felt a little shocked when her mother told her she sometimes felt like slamming her children against the wall. Mom seemed like she might have been sort of disturbed by the idea. Maybe that's why she's never told me whether or not she ever felt like slamming me against a wall. The thing is, if she ever did, I would understand, now that I am a mother myself.

Somehow, almost right after my first baby came out, so did my first major appearances of anger. I am not entirely sure where that anger came from. Perhaps it had been hiding inside somewhere waiting for an outlet or maybe it spontaneously combusted somehow, but there it was—right in my face, squalling and ugly. I would not be accurate if I said I never felt angry before I had my first child, but I can certainly say I never felt anger as intensely or as often as I have after becoming a mother.

I had no idea what I was supposed to do with the frightening flare-ups of frustration I began to experience. I didn't have any weapons with which to attack the dragon of maternal anger whenever it reared its ugly head. I could, as women love to do, explain and excuse my feelings and behavior on hormones, or lack of sleep. Certainly these things were factors in my angry outbursts, but they were not the source of them. I have just recently come to realize that physical factors just take the lid off the junk inside us. They don't usually put it there.

Darkening the sunshiny delight of the new love in my life were the scary shadows of anger. I was so crazy about our child. Why did I go crazy with anger sometimes? Anger usually stems back to pain of some sort, either physical or emotional. Much of the anger I felt during the early months of mothering were related to the torturous nursing sessions I forced myself to endure. As time went on my triggers moved around to whatever was a source of frustration at the time – wriggliness, neediness, clinginess, whininess, stubbornness, hyperness, nothing unique to Tim. Nothing that every mother doesn't have to deal with.

Once we get free from anger's life-sucking grip on us, we may find ourselves wondering what our problem was. I am still not exactly sure, and I am still not perfectly free, but I can say this—Ripping off and throwing away the leech of anger is one of the best gifts a mother can ever give her family and her self. Anger sucks our blood—our love, our strength, our health, our joy. Anger is sometimes referred to as a passion because it is a strong feeling, but it is usually a passion that weakens love, not one that strengthens it. Every time I have squeezed too hard, yelled too loudly, spoken too sharply, or dripped sarcasm, we were all drained. My children were not the problem. They were victims of my problem.

A strange thing about mothers is that we tend to protect our children fiercely but are sometimes oblivious to the effects of our own hurtful actions, words, or emotions. In fact, by virtue of our extremely crucial role in their lives, we can inflict more damage on them than anyone else who says or does the same sorts of things. A clerk at McDonald's was quite rude to Tim once and I found myself seething inside at her snappiness at an innocent child, until I realized that I was just as bad if not worse at times. Maybe that was the day I began to grasp the concept of using my maternal protection instinct to attack the anger that was hurting us. Anger disguises itself as an outlet for frustration and pain, when it is really a furnace for more. Angry outbursts don't relieve us, they rob us—of energy, joy, and peace.

My anger problems with Tim began within weeks of his birth and peaked at the end of a particularly long winter when he was a rather intense fifteen-month-old, no doubt reflecting my own intensity with him. One major issue at that time, which sounds ridiculous now, was keys. Little Timmy was very adamant about wanting to open car doors and the house door with my keys. (Being new at the business, I thought it was nice to let him learn new things and didn't foresee any potential difficulties in letting him try to use keys.) Soon, Timmy came to insist, with loud shrieks, on being allowed to always put the keys in the car or house. Of course, he was unable to actually open the doors even if he could find the right key and get it in. Then he would crumple in rage and frustration when I would have to pry the keys away from him and open the door myself. Now that I've gained a decade of experience and perspective, I can see a number of solutions to solve that problem (which should never have gotten so major) but back then it was a big, frustrating, unfixable deal.

I have one of those ingrained-in-my-memory sorts of pictures of Timmy in my arms in the backseat of our old car in the underground parking lot of a grocery store. Exhausted from a long shopping trip with a wiggly one-year-old, I was trying to get groceries in the car and get home. The wiggly one-year-old, however, was focused on putting the keys in the car door and was becoming increasingly frustrated, as was I. Knowing he couldn't get the door open himself, I took the keys so I could get the groceries in the car. Predictably, Tim went into a fit of frustration, and I followed suit. I tried to stuff him into his car seat too forcefully and accidentally bumped his head on the top of the car. Trying to comfort a child while you are feeling both guilty and angry is very emotionally challenging. I just sort of crumpled into the backseat, defeated and drained, with Timmy crying on my lap, frustrated and hurt. I caught a glimpse of the two of us together in the rear-view mirror, both so young, both so upset and both so afraid of our own and each other's intensity.

Now that I have perspective on this time of my life, I can see the symptoms of post-partum depression—insomnia, deep and dark sadness, lack of hope, unexplained physical pain, flares of anger. I can even remember lying in bed one day shortly after having Tim and very briefly thinking of suicide, then dismissing it since it wouldn't be good for the baby or Herb. I'm not sure why I was surprised when I learned about the direct link between anger and depression. I knew them both well in the early years of my mothering. They fed off each other inside of me, strengthening each other and weakening me.

I have been better at managing my emotions with Daniel than I was with Tim. To begin with, I did not start out mothering him carrying a burdensome backpack of low-grade post-partum depression. In fact, the reason I even came to realize I had been carrying it the first time is that I didn't have it the second time and felt so much lighter. I have also learned some lessons about self-control, self-pity (the number one enemy of joy), and things like the importance of getting some time away from the children, however brief. There have certainly been some tough spells, and some incidents that I am not at all proud of, but the leeches are losing. And my whole family is gaining.

Julie Ann Barnhill wrote a book titled "She's Gonna Blow" in which she shares her struggles with, and eventual victory over, maternal anger.[1] As Julie began to share on the subject at mother's conferences, organizers found that her seminars filled up exceptionally fast. Very rarely do you find a mother who is completely free from the harmful effects of some form of anger, and very rarely do you find a mother who doesn't want to get rid of a bloodsucker. Sometimes anger leeches stay fairly small. Other times they can become almost all encompassing. The good news is that no matter how big our leech has grown, we are always bigger. With God on our side, we can and will win.

When Daniel was a toddler, Tim got lots of kicks out of his little brother's antics. My annoyance over whatever Daniel had gotten into was often airbrushed by Tim's delighted giggles. Tim used to affectionately call Daniel "a pack of trouble", which was a pretty good nickname for a pretty long while. He really liked to get into the large flour and sugar canisters in the kitchen, sprinkling and sampling the contents, as well as planting miscellaneous objects therein. I have a vivid memory of going to get some sugar and finding an entire box of S.O.S scouring pads, in very flaky form, that Daniel had found under the sink and dumped into the sugar canister.

I think most mothers would say it is not the one-time sorts of incidents like this that cause mothers to blow as much as the on-going incidents and demands that can build to volcanic proportions if a mother doesn't have healthy outlets. An isolated incident, like Daniel drawing on the walls with permanent marker when my back was turned, can turn into a story to tell someone, or can at least be something to internally point to as a reason for why we feel so steamy. Too many dirty diapers a day, too much fighting over toys, too many demands, too much laundry, too little time, too many spills, too much whining—these are the things that can create some serious deposits of frustration. These sorts of things we need to accept as natural byproducts of childhood, manage the best we can, and get ourselves at least a little break from.

I do not know how many times I have had to apologize to our children over the past dozen years. They have always forgiven me with the amazing grace a child gives. Once I went to Tim to apologize for being angry after I had cooled off from whatever had set me off. I believe paint was involved. He said to me, "I knew you would do that. I knew you would do that in the end." He was little then and the forgiveness flowed freely. He's getting into his preteen years now and is beginning to brood a little. Not long ago, he was up in his bunk alone stewing over something I'd said to him and when I went in to apologize he told me, "I was thinking. No matter what, you're still my Mom." I told him that God loves us like that only a whole lot more. It's funny that I can't remember the incidents that prompted these conversations. The rottenness has been removed and only the sweetness remains. As the Good Book says, love covers over a multitude of sins.

One late afternoon I was grocery shopping with the boys before supper, which is indisputably their most hyper time of day. I went into the outing in an uptight sort of mood and was not exactly enjoying the excursion with two bouncing boys. Then Tim dropped a whole watermelon on the floor while he was trying to weigh it. It did not land safely, to say the least. Miraculously, I laughed. A few years before I would have exploded right after the watermelon did, or hissed and seethed since we were in public, but I just burst out laughing. Tim looked very afraid at the sight of the splattered melon, then very relieved at my reaction. "Sometimes you have to either laugh or cry," I told him later. I'm thankful I was able to laugh. I have come a long way, and I am going to keep going.

Getting rid of leeches can be challenging and sometimes downright painful. I've read books on anger, and tried to get more sleep, more exercise, and more time to myself. These sorts of things certainly help to ease anger, but they can't cure it. The deep-down antidote for anger is forgiveness. If we can forgive the wrongs from our past and our present, if we can ask for forgiveness when we need to, and if we can forgive ourselves without excusing ourselves, our anger will shrivel up and fall off like a lake leech doused in salt. The victories will be sweet.

Sherry's Story

When Sherry was two years old she moved back in with her mother. She and her older sister had been living with another family for several months while their mother tried to get her life in order. Unfortunately for Sherry, her sister, and a brother who came along later, their mother didn't get, or didn't stay, in good enough working order. Sherry's mother's addictions kept her from caring for her children properly and they were often left to fend for themselves with what little they could find around the house.

When Sherry was about five she began hanging around the local rock quarry with a number of children from similar sorts of situations. "We had a potluck every night," she tells me with the sense of humor that often develops in people who have suffered and survived. The kids would all bring whatever they could find around their houses while their stoned or drunk parents were not watching, then share it among their community of neglect. Sometimes the children would get caught taking cans of food, and would be beaten for "stealing" what they needed to survive.

When Sherry was six and a half, someone began bringing cigarettes to share and she started to smoke. When she was seven, she tried the alcohol and pot that the older kids brought to the quarry. By the time she was thirteen, Sherry was a full-blown alcoholic. She went from having straight A's all the way from kindergarten through sixth grade to having D's in junior high. "I couldn't function without a bar in the top of my locker," she said. In a school of about two hundred students, Sherry felt ignored and alone. All of her friends had dropped out of school and the teachers seemed to care only about the "good" students.

Sherry developed a protective who-cares-about-the-world sort of attitude and began to depend completely upon her circle of "friends" from similar situations. Escalating tension at home resulted in Sherry getting kicked out when she was just fifteen. She had nowhere to go and it was winter—far too cold to sleep at the rock quarry. In the evenings, after the small town's post office closed for the night, Sherry would sleep inside the foyer doors until slightly before the office opened again in the mornings, when she would slip out undetected. After a week of sleeping in the post office, Sherry found a friend to take her in, and then continued living at various older friends' houses for about three years.

During the time she lived with friends, she met a man about ten years older than she was, who had a child from a previous relationship. Over time, she began sleeping with him and found out she was pregnant the day after her eighteenth birthday, three months after she graduated from high school. Her boyfriend didn't react with great joy when he found out from a cousin that Sherry was pregnant. Sherry had been planning on telling him about the pregnancy but hadn't gotten the chance. By the time Sherry was six months pregnant, the "father" of her child had entirely disappeared and disconnected his phone.

Her small town's rumor mill got ahead of Sherry again when her parents heard from someone else that their daughter was pregnant. They weren't thrilled either. Sherry's mother and stepfather wanted her to get an abortion and drove her into the closest city for all the preparatory appointments. The day they brought her in for the actual abortion Sherry says they "made one mistake." They just dropped her off, instead of bringing her into the office. Sherry walked away from the clinic, and kept walking with no particular destination in mind. She eventually found herself at the home of some long-term friends of her family, Steve and Janet. Janet is the daughter of the woman who took care of Sherry as an unofficial foster mother when she was little. The relationship between the two families has continued through the many years since Sherry's mother first called a pregnancy distress line and talked with Janet's mother. Though Sherry had not been made aware of her parents' arrangements, plans had been made for her to stay with Steve and Janet while she was recuperating from the abortion.

Steve and Janet welcomed Sherry into their home for the remainder of her pregnancy and helped her begin a new life. Janet was also expecting her first child and went through a difficult delivery just six weeks before Sherry had her baby with little trouble. Janet had a boy and Sherry had a girl, whom she named Kaylee. Janet became a real-life mother model for Sherry. Janet was someone to learn from as well as someone to keep her company throughout the intense first weeks of early motherhood. "Before I started hanging around with Steve and Janet, I didn't know how to talk," Sherry said. Conversation in the quarry, or with drunk or stoned friends, was probably limited and repetitive. Steve and Janet's friendship has helped to bring Sherry into a very different sort of world.

Two years before becoming a mother, Sherry had attempted suicide, driven to desperation from all the turmoil in her life. Before she was allowed out of the hospital she was required to complete an anger management program with a psychologist. The coping skills she learned from the program gave her the emotional tools she's needed to deal with her little daughter, and all the other things life brings that could create outbursts of rage. Unfortunately, one week after being released from the hospital, Sherry's family home burned down and she lost everything she had been keeping there, including her papers from the anger management program. "I wish I could thank him," she said of the doctor who brought her through the program.

In spite of all the indications against her success as a mother, Sherry is a responsible, committed, and caring mother to her little daughter. She has been strong enough not to pass on the neglect and anger she suffered in her own childhood and youth. Another extremely remarkable success of Sherry's is her ability to overcome the alcoholism that had already gotten hold of her by the age of thirteen. While Sherry drank heavily during the early part of her pregnancy, she was able to quit drinking for the baby's sake and Kaylee is free from any symptoms of fetal alcohol syndrome. Since having Kaylee, Sherry has spent some time with friends who were drinking and just wasn't interested in it anymore. She was also able to quit smoking during her pregnancy. After Kaylee was born, Sherry sometimes cut herself as an outlet for her inner pain, but found the motivation to stop cutting by asking herself, "What would Kaylee think?"

When Kaylee was two months old Sherry moved out of Steve and Janet's house and into her own apartment. During the early months of Kaylee's life, Sherry didn't feel any strong attachments to her child and found herself thinking, "I don't love this child. There's no reason I should keep her." But she did keep looking after her faithfully and after about six months she got too attached to Kaylee to make any adoption plans. She found herself not wanting to go anywhere without her daughter, and she loved to watch Kaylee crawl and hear her talk. When I asked Sherry what she finds hard about being a mother she said, "Being with her, but also being away from her."

For a number of months Sherry worked at a daycare until the center she was working at closed down. She then found work at a used clothing store, waking at five in the morning to catch the bus to her work and arriving home after seven o'clock at night. Kaylee developed a number of health issues and seemed to be on antibiotics for well over a year. Sherry worries about her daughter's health and also about their financial situation. She feels like she is always struggling to have enough money for rent, groceries and the things Kaylee needs.

I met Sherry at Steve and Janet's house, where she used to go every Tuesday night for supper for more than a year after moving into her own place. Kaylee was thirteen months old at the time and toddled trustingly to her mother, hunting for her after playing in another room with Janet's baby for a while. I asked Sherry what she enjoys about being Kaylee's mother. "Playing with her," she said. "I never really got to have a childhood."

Chapter 4

A Matter of Life or Not

While I was going through my pregnancy with Daniel, I had sort of settled on the fact that this would be our last child but immediately after I was delivered, the buried question began to stick its neck out: *Will this really be our last?* The wondering started to sound while I lay bleeding on the delivery bed. It echoed with an increasing insistency while I packed away but held onto maternity and baby clothes, while I watched our rapidly-growing baby wriggle on his change table, and while I weaned him. For many months, the question just swirled around inside of me, unprocessed. I was too tired and busy to think it through properly. Then late one winter night I picked up a blank book with a picture of a baby's bare foot on it and wrote this:

> ***February 27th***
>
> Two years ago today I threw up for the first time (definitely not the last) in a long-awaited pregnancy.
>
> Today, I will think through more thoroughly the question that's been rumbling around my mind ever since Daniel's been born: Is he our last?

As I started to think about that question, I realized the question I needed to be asking myself was not "Do I want more children?" but "Does God want us to have more children?" Then I asked myself, "Why do I want more children?" Beginning to honestly answer that question resulted in me getting sort of stuck for almost a year. On Timothy's eighth birthday I re-opened that book and that question, asking God to take away all my wrong reasons for wanting another child, and to replace them with right reasons. Since this part of my motherhood journey is still unfolding, I've decided that the best way to tell about what happened next, and what has yet to happen, is to share some snatches from that journal.

January 19th

You can make many plans, but the Lord's purpose will prevail.

Proverbs 19:21

February 13th

Fatigue, sickness, weakness, insomnia, irritability, weepiness, back pain, night wakes, bleeding hemorrhoids, discouragement, negativity, infections, aches, breast pain, plugged ducts, shortness of breath, sciatic spasms, ever-present nausea, dehydration, faintness, dizziness, lack of energy, leg cramps, weight gain, feeling fat and ugly…

I am considering the physical cost of having a birth child. Realized today that so far in my life I haven't yet really made a conscious choice to sacrifice for God's, or anyone else's, sake.

February 19th

"I will lead you and guide you in wisdom from above. All things will be as I plan them, if you allow Me the freedom to shape circumstances and lead you to the right decisions. I am merciful and kind. I love you beyond measure…

I want you to prosper and be in health. I want you to know Me more intimately. If difficulties come, it is by My order and for your benefit. Others would say you have trouble: I would say you have a test."[1]

He might test you, to do you good in the end.

Deuteronomy 8:16

I may be tested to see:

a) If I will let go of my own desires and accept Your will of no more children for us.

b) If I can accept, love, and serve any child You bring to our family through adoption.

c) If I can deal with the physical and emotional challenges of pregnancy and postpartum with courage and grace.

d) If I will continue to follow faithfully if I think we are being led in a particular direction and are blocked.

e) If I will choose joy, peace, faithfulness, and self-control in the face of trials, disappointments, or long-term difficulties.

Whatever happens in the days to come, may I be found faithful.

February 21st

"I direct every motion of your life, as the ocean bears a ship. Your will and intelligence may be at the helm, but divine providence and sovereignty are stronger forces. You can trust Me, knowing that any pressure I bring to bear upon your life is initiated by My love, and I will not do even this except as you are willing and desire.

Many a ship has sailed from port to port with no interference from Me, because Strong Will has been at the wheel. Multitudes of pleasure cruises go merrily on their ways, untouched by the power of My hand. But you have put your life into My keeping, and because you are depending on Me for guidance and direction, I shall give it."[2]

February 25th

Both in my reading and in my real-life observations, I have recently come to notice that it seems to be the mother who usually initiates the wanting and working for a child. She often needs to pull the father along, like the mother wolf on

Disney's *Jungle Book* movie giving a certain look to the father wolf that led to their taking in Mowgli. Why is this?

The mother is the bridge between father and child – the man loves the woman, the woman bears the child? Because the mother must suffer more so she is given a stronger desire?

April 9th

I have recently come back from a writer's conference and decided that since it took nine months for a publishing house to think about reading one of my projects, only to turn it down without even reading it, I should certainly be able to squeeze having a baby in without missing much in the book industry. An author named Terri Camp, who I sat with at dinner one night, has also inspired me. She has eight children, was sick every time she was pregnant, and has somehow managed to write and publish books. She generously gave me two of her books to take home and I read them on the airplane, feeling rather wimpy about my worries.

Also at the conference was a woman named Barbara Curtis, who has twelve children, three of which have Down's Syndrome. She manages to get many articles written, published, and awarded. I did not actually get to talk with her but I could tell from far off that nothing ruffles her much. She says she has just learned to write in the midst of her family. I am taking these walking testimonies as living proof that God will give us everything we need to do everything He wants us to do. This fact can be not only inexplicable but downright miraculous sometimes.

I have been thinking about having another child as something to do, something to be able to manage. Now I must begin to see him or her as someone to love.

April 12th

Realized in the last few days that I could experience deep, long-term regret over not having another child if I didn't have one only because it was easier not to. I have been worrying that I might regret the decision to have another child, forgetting that I could have far deeper regrets about deciding not to have one. This has to be Your decision. It can't be about me. It has to be about You, and what You want.

April 16th

This afternoon I talked with a worker from the adoption agency I like and found out their fee is flat for Canadians. This makes this option more viable.

"In all your ways acknowledge Him and He shall direct your paths." PROVERBS 3:6

April 17th

Last night I dreamt of a baby, alive and moving inside of me, and I loved it with my whole heart once I realized it was there.

April 26th

Tonight we officially decided to try for another birth baby. We've been heading in this direction for a while I guess. We didn't seem to be able to agree on how to go about adopting even though we were both open to the idea. In Herb's mind, we'd already decided to walk down the birth child path, but tonight is the night it sinks into my head. It's been in my heart quite some time already. I just needed some confirmation. Actually, I needed a lot of confirmation.

O My children, the path where I will lead you is not easy for your human nature to bear. It is not a pleasant way, nor in accord with your selfish desires...

Like a flood, I will cause the tears to flow through you, and I will purge out your self-life; and I will give you My love."[3]

Pam's Story

"You sound sick," I remarked to Pam one weekend evening when she and her family arrived at our place for supper.

"Do I?" she asked. After thinking for a minute she replied, "Yeah, I guess I am."

This is a typical sort of attitude for Pam. She doesn't focus much on how she's feeling, or think much about what would be best for her own interests. Pam is a purposely sacrificial person—strong enough to willingly give of her time, energy, sleep, peace and quiet for the greater good. Pam is one of the least selfish people I have ever met so I was rather surprised at her response when I asked her how motherhood has changed her and she immediately answered, "Realizing how selfish I am."

Pam had her first baby, Jake, on December 31st after making a very touching appearance as Mary in our Christmas pageant that year. Throughout her first night with Jake she held him in her arms all night because she couldn't reach the call button to ask for help with putting him somewhere else. After awhile, she decided she didn't want to move him anyway.

Pam felt isolated in the early stages of her mothering. The many things she was doing before having Jake ended rather rapidly, her apartment was far from any friends or family, and she did not have a vehicle to get around in. "There were days I was glad to go and get the mail," she said. Pam felt happy to be a mother though, and remembers thinking to herself very early on, "I like this". She became pregnant again when Jake was just nine months old and was pleased to be having another child.

When I asked Pam what becoming a mother was like she said, "I've been trying to think about that. I guess it was like when a natural disaster comes in and completely changes your world." She had packed her first pregnancy full with work, taking classes, and teaching classes that all ended at Christmas, shortly before her due date. "I was anticipating the end of life," she commented, knowing now what she could only suspect then. The coming of a child brings about the end of life without that child, but it births something altogether new and wonderful.

In the fourth month of her second pregnancy Pam started bleeding, having contractions, and feeling very cold. She providentially happened to have a doctor's appointment already booked for that morning. When Pam told her doctor about the bleeding and contractions the doctor told her she was losing the baby. Pam blamed herself for over-exercising and working too hard in preparation for the move they were about to make. She lay on her couch for four hours that day, even though she felt she had already lost or was in the process of losing the baby. When an ultrasound technician assured her, "The baby is doing fine," during an ultrasound exam, Pam's temperature immediately went up. She figures she was in a state of shock and the relief of her baby being still alive brought her out of that state. As was later discovered, what was actually causing her bleeding was the placenta tearing away from the wall of the uterus. Over time, a very rare condition called *Vasa Previa* was detected in which the placenta splits into two sections with blood vessels connecting the two halves.

Because it was impossible to detect how big the connecting blood vessels were, doctors did not want Pam to go into labor at all. If the blood vessels were large, there was significant danger of fatal hemorrhaging for both Pam and her baby. Pam's pregnancy was riddled with medical tests, questions, and the unknown. One day as she was getting into her car she wondered, "Should I really be driving? What if I get in an accident?" Pam told me each of her pregnancies taught her a distinct lesson and this one's was: *I can take reasonable measures, but I do not have control and am not ultimately responsible. I cannot control the life or death of a child.* Essentially, Pam kept learning this lesson during each pregnancy, in different and increasingly deeper ways.

Pam had a scheduled Caesarean delivery two weeks before her due date even though the baby didn't seem quite ready. Baby Abigail came into the outside world weighing five pounds, three ounces and was promptly ignored by the swarms of medical staff, who rushed to examine and take pictures of the placenta, a medical novelty. One blood vessel connecting the two sections of the placenta was as thick as the umbilical cord and would certainly have caused almost immediate death for the baby and severe hemorrhaging for Pam if it had ruptured. Pam is very thankful for the technician who caught the problem early in her pregnancy. Quite some time after Abby's safe delivery, Pam's doctor told her that she had hardly slept the last few weeks of the pregnancy due to her worry and stress over Pam's situation.

Having two very small children, recovering from her Caesarean, and moving into a new house all at the same time didn't seem to daunt Pam much. "I like a challenge," she said. She's in the right job—motherhood offers plenty of challenges. Not everyone notices them, or rises to them, but Pam embraces them with open arms, encompassing not only her own children, but many others as well. She has been working with the children of our church ever since I can remember. She also baby-sits during the week and often watches other people's kids when their parents need help of some sort.

Whenever I talk to Pam on the phone I wonder how she manages to carry on any sort of conversation, let alone be as clear-minded as she is, with different degrees of chaos going on around her. We had an interesting conversation one time with both of our sons playing their recorders in the not-very-background. Another time she interrupted herself to say smoothly to one of the boys she baby-sits, "Just leave it. I'll vacuum it later. Oh – were you trying to fish?". I marvel at Pam's unflappable patience. She is one of those people who teaches things without trying to.

When Pam's third pregnancy was made public at church I was both surprised and strangely elated. I heard of it in a roundabout sort of way since she and I were both downstairs with our respective gaggles of children while the news was circulating upstairs. Since Pam and Trevor already had a boy and a girl up and running, I assumed this pregnancy was what is traditionally referred to as an "accident". It wasn't, I found out later, but was the result of many months of internal debate and desire. Perhaps one reason I thrilled at this development is that I was beginning to let myself entertain this exact same sort of question – to have or not to have.

When Pam was pregnant I was concerned for her. Every week she got bigger and wearier but kept hauling around two and three year old children even though her back was bothering her. She was home schooling Jake for the year, and Abby was just coming out of an intensely clingy and tantrummy stage. Pam was constantly at the church doing something or other. I tried to tell her, in the indirect way women have of communicating with each other, to take care of herself. I'm not sure she heard me but she has not only survived but thrived. "There are days I'm just exhausted," Pam says, "but I know I'm called to do what I'm doing and I know God will give me the strength I need to do it."

When Pam was trying to decide whether or not they should have a third child, all the reasons she could think of to not have another were "all selfish"—things such as wanting more time for herself to exercise or read. Trevor was not very sold on the concept of another child but assented in time, probably due to Pam telling him, "I really, really want another baby." Then as soon as she found out she was pregnant, Pam panicked and began to wrestle with questions that caused her to feel somewhat numb throughout her pregnancy. When she was in pain during labor her doubts intensified and she wondered why she ever wanted a third child. Her one relief was Trevor telling her jokes (I have no idea what jokes can possibly be funny during labor—I didn't ask).

Doubts and distress turned rapidly into joy as soon as Aydan came into her arms. Aydan is an absolutely beautiful boy with angel-blonde hair, extremely endearing dimples, and very blue eyes. Pam and I sat together in a tent at an outdoor wedding shortly after Aydan was born. She laid him in her lap and we feasted our eyes on his soul-deep beauty. "It's all worth it, isn't it?" I asked her, knowing the answer.

"Yes."

Lately, I've been experiencing what I can only refer to as "Mommy crushes", a heartmelt sort of sensation at the sight of certain children. These crushes strike at random and without notice. By noticing the looks on other mothers faces sometimes, I believe I am not alone in these tenderness attacks. Mine are most often triggered by boys (of any age) and can be a one-time sort of thing, or ongoing, as in Aydan's case. Pam was over a few months ago for a "play date" (mostly for the mothers) and the tenderness Aydan evoked in me crawling around and getting into things was almost disconcerting. "What do I do with this feeling?" I asked God later.

"Keep it," He advised.

Aydan has grown rapidly into a typical little troublemaker. We were all over at our friends' very new house a while ago and Aydan somehow located an electric mixer. Since it didn't have the beaters in, Aydan took it to be an iron and used it to iron the hardwood kitchen floor. He looked remarkably cute and everybody just stood around and watched him for quite a while. I believe the homeowners even took pictures. They are, thankfully, very gracious people since Abby and Daniel came very close to breaking a glass china cabinet with a baseball bat. They also made rather a lot of noise that night slamming doors. "Oh, the doors were made to be used," the hosts said kindly when I apologized. They told Aydan, "You can come and iron our floors anytime."

It is quite touching for me to watch Trevor's tenderness for his little boy, this child he didn't think they could manage. "We've moved from man-to-man to zone defense," he told Herb, a statement which Herb had to explain to me later. Trevor is clearly crazy about his new child, and seems to have gained an even deeper appreciation for Pam. "My wife is an incredible woman," Trevor said when he spoke in our church on Mother's Day. She is.

I tell Pam's story not because it is particularly dramatic or even much out of the ordinary, as far as plot goes. Apart from her lottery-odd placenta experience, Pam's life is pretty regular-looking on the outside. Her days overflow with childcare, laundry, dishes, volunteering at church and school, and correspondence courses. But on the inside Pam is anything but common. She radiates a warmth that is a reflection of her heart-fire within. Everyone who comes anywhere near her can't help but feel it.

One evening after all our kids were supposed to be in bed I went to Pam's house for an uninterrupted visit. Aydan somehow snuck back upstairs for some more snuggling, but neither of us minded. As we chatted quietly he drifted off, his eyelids fluttering against his will, and his tiny toes poking out of his sleeper. Pam was wearing a sweater that was frayed all around the cuffs and had her dark hair pulled up. As I looked at her there on her couch I wondered if she knew she was beautiful—a raven-haired Madonna.

There is something incomparably beautiful about motherhood that we have somehow become unconscious of. I don't believe men are blind to that beauty, but it seems as though women have often self-surrendered the honor that should accompany one who bears and cares for a child. Instead, we focus on relatively meaningless things like fitting back into our jeans or trying to make sure we don't "let ourselves go"; as though beauty is something you can buy at a hair salon.

What if we started "taking care" of ourselves by tending not only our bodies but also our hearts and souls? What if we didn't resist the changes motherhood brings, but embraced them? I believe we would become increasingly beautiful as we let ourselves change and give and love—unafraid of losing our value, and confident in gaining greater and greater beauty as the years go by.

On Fear and Change

We've been checking out middle schools for Tim this past month. Next year he will be starting a bigger school with bigger kids and bigger issues. I was three grades older than Tim when I had to make a similar sort of change, and I remember dreading it. Change usually involves at least a little fear, so people tend to resist change even if it's a good change, and even if we aren't pre-teens.

We tend to feel anxious about what we haven't experienced yet, about what we cannot see, and about what we do not understand. Stress experts say even good change is stressful—probably because it involves experiencing something unfamiliar to us. During my growing up years our family had cattle. When calves were born outside in bad weather we used to try to get them and their mothers into the barn for shelter. This, let me assure you, was easier said than done. Even though we wanted a good change for the calves they almost always resisted it, locking their legs and having to be pushed or carried most of the way. I guess I'm not one to talk. I've been feeling pretty lock-legged over this change on the horizon, this child that will change our family, our routines, our transportation and sleeping arrangements. No one is pushing me to have this child so I have nobody to resist. Nothing short of plain old fear of change is locking my legs.

Not very long ago, Herb felt God was leading him to resign from his senior management position and take a part-time hourly job in order to have more time for our family and for church work. I was in agreement with this major work change but nervous about it, not for financial reasons but for relational ones. I was used to being with the boys almost all the time since Herb worked long days and often had meetings at night. He was also gone on trips fairly often so I had developed my own ways of managing things that felt like they worked well for me. I was afraid Herb and I would start getting in each other's hair, that he would start being stingy, and that I would miss the boys during the times I was to be working on my writing in another part of the house. Then the little fears of getting on each other's nerves grew, as fears do, into fears of serious marriage problems, serious family problems, and serious financial problems. Seriously, it was silly.

I decided to go along with the work change plan cheerfully for Herb's sake, who was becoming very worn out from the demands of work and church leadership and had very little time or energy left for himself or our family. After the plan came to life, I was surprised by how much I loved it. I feared the change but now that the change has come to life, I have welcomed it warmly and am very thankful for it. I have a feeling there may be some parallels for me to pick up on here.

It is not as though the concept of having another child is a new one for me, nor an unwelcome one. Even while I was still pregnant with Daniel I felt sad about the probability of it being my last pregnancy. I didn't want to be done having children yet. I didn't feel done (there does come a time when a woman seems to just know she is done) but I felt that, all things considered, I probably should be done.

Late one night a couple of months after Daniel was born we were traveling back home on a fourteen hour drive from Herb's parents place. The boys were both sleeping in the back and it was a rare moment of complete peace. Herb shocked me by bringing up the question of whether or not we would be having any more children. Previously, it always had to be me to bring up anything in the family planning department so I was quite pleased by the very fact that he asked the question that had been swirling around my mind for months.

When Herb brought this subject up, his witnessing of my suffering during pregnancy and birth were fresh in his mind. He was also tired out from late-night lunch shifts. After some discussion, he said he didn't feel we should have any more birth children, but that we could maybe think about adopting later. Though I could see the wisdom in this I still felt sorrow and disappointment despite the vow I had made to myself in the midst of my illness with Daniel. I remember this desperate moment very clearly. In a bad bout of nauseous insomnia, I came out to the couch in the middle of the night again and lay there awake, feeling as gross as I had ever felt in my life. "I am never doing this again," I promised myself.

After giving birth to Daniel I lay flat and shaking on the hospital bed, still in pain that I couldn't do anything about. I comforted myself by thinking, "I never have to do this again." Looking back, I realize this statement was already reflecting a change of heart since my earlier vow in the throes of vomiting. My message to myself had changed from "I am never doing this again" to "I do not have to do this again."

Of all the factors that are making my legs lock at the thought of another birth child, it is the sickness that is the strongest. "Morning sickness" is such a poor term for what some of us go through during pregnancy. The MotherRisk Centre here in Canada is trying to get a new name going which is far better, in my opinion. They refer to the condition as "NVP" which is short for "nausea and vomiting during pregnancy." It hasn't caught on too well yet. Anyway, Herb has now officially changed his mind about having another birth child. Actually, if I know Herb, he probably doesn't even remember our previous conversation in the van. Time does heal, or at least lends the perspective (or the forgetfulness) that we need sometimes to be able to move forward. This is how women get themselves pregnant again. We literally forget about the pain and by the time we remember, it's too late. Then by the time the pain's over, we're not sorry after all.

One of our major concerns in the third child issue is our second child. Daniel will become a middle child, which may be especially difficult if the baby is another boy. How will he handle a new sibling? Will he feel left out, unwanted, displaced, or hurt? Will he think we tried again because he wasn't good enough? Will he become difficult to deal with? Unlike Tim at his age, Daniel hasn't shown much interest in having a little brother or sister. Maybe it's because he has an older brother and hasn't thought much about having a younger one.

As far as Tim is concerned, he has wanted more babies in our family from the very day Daniel was born. Since he is immune to any suffering in the addition of children to our family, he is gung ho for more since he quite likes younger children. When he was little, he wanted to be a mailman who had seventeen children. I think he may have revised that plan a little already. After Daniel was born Tim kept telling us to have a baby every five years until there were four boys in our family, just like Daddy's family. The difference would be that Tim would be fifteen when his youngest brother was born. His Daddy was just six when his third brother was born, pretty much the age Tim was when he got his first.

For what seemed like a long time Timmy was the special little guy, the only child not only in our own family but also in both families at large. Now he is the special big guy with a rapidly increasing crop of cousins who follow him around and crawl all over him.

Tim makes the perfect oldest child since he genuinely likes babies and little kids, and is really quite a patient person—a trait I won't try to take credit for.

One morning last week I was still lying in bed at seven o'clock when Tim got up. He saw me lying there awake and asked in a very hopeful tone, "Are you feeling sick?" He is on the alert for signs of an impending baby. He has been both praying and pestering for one for quite some time now. I am hoping to have the chance to tell him some good news sometime. Hopefully his excitement will buoy his little brother for the storms ahead. I think most of our family and friends will be surprised when we tell them our news. They've probably all concluded we're not going to have any more children, which is the logical thing to conclude given our circumstances not to mention our ages. I know my Mom has wanted a girl for us but I think she has more or less given up. Since she had a girl and a boy she wants me to be able to experience having both genders too.

Herb's Mom is quite amazing with boys. She has somehow maintained her gracious femininity after living with five males for several decades. I am just now beginning to understand why she was so excited when I came into the family after thirty-two years. She wanted some company! After having seven boys in a row (four sons and three grandsons) Mom got a little granddaughter, Aliah. When I congratulated her on finally getting a girl in the family she said warmly, "Everyone's special." Personally, I probably would have thrown some sort of party and bought everything pink within a ten mile radius.

When I first started thinking about having another child I really wanted to have a girl to the extent that I didn't think I would handle having another boy well. At the time, the boys were going through a stage that involved a lot of wrestling and burping, and I thought I would feel overwhelmed by the increasingly loud male factor. Now, those fears have disappeared somehow and all I want is a child.

Truth be told, I rather like boys, loud as they are sometimes. If we have another boy birth child I know some people will feel sorry for us, assuming we were aiming for a girl. But we won't feel sorry at all. We'll have gotten what we wanted—someone to love.

The stretching that changes bring about in our lives can sometimes feel quite uncomfortable, but the increased flexibility and strength those stretches grant us are worth the initial discomforts. Stretching actually hurts less than seizing, and is less stressful than the pressure of maintaining a leg-lock as we are pushed or carried somewhere bigger and better. Our lives will constantly be changing whether or not we make any effort to change them—change is a symptom of being alive.

A mother's fears certainly aren't limited to things that involve change. We may fear rare or not-so-rare diseases, freak accidents, terrorists, sexual abuse, schoolyard bullies, learning disabilities, or wrong crowds. Whether or not these sorts of fears ever materialize, we need to face them. Modern motherhood requires both courage and faith. We can't let our fears darken our days, dampen our delight in our children, or keep us from doing something important.

Jennifer's Story

As the eighth of nine children growing up in a rural Kenyan village, Jennifer was poor in the material sense, but didn't become aware of any economic lack until later in life. She had a rich, happy childhood full of freedom and friends to play with and was largely immune to the struggles the adult members of her family faced. Since most of the fifty or sixty families living in Jennifer's village had eight or nine children, whatever Jennifer unknowingly lacked in toys and treats was made up for in plenty of playmates and lots of room to run.

Jennifer's father was one of the national leaders who were very vocal about the need for the British colonial government to give Kenya its independence. He was detained in prison for seven years along with other Kikuyu leaders before being released when the country finally gained its independence in 1963. By that time, his family's property was gone, but his older children had been sent to high school on the generosity of others from the village. When the British government handed over power to African leaders, it seemed they appointed only those whom they felt would be easy to influence. Jennifer's father did not qualify and had to immediately look for a menial job in a city away from his family, where he lived on cornbread and red pepper stew. Jennifer believes this diet, coupled with the stress of his years in detention, caused her father to develop serious stomach ulcers, which led to his death when Jennifer was just eight years old.

After her father's death, Jennifer's mother had to work long hours on a neighboring coffee and vegetable farm. Jennifer's grandmother cared for Jennifer, her five sisters, and her three brothers until the children grew old enough to care for themselves. Thanks to their mother's income from the coffee garden, Jennifer's older brothers were the first ones from her village to get a university degree. Jennifer followed in her older sibling's footsteps and began boarding school for ninth grade. This was when she first noticed that her family was not as financially privileged as other families. Even though all the girls wore uniforms, their personal belongings in their rooms reflected a different standard of living than Jennifer had come from.

After graduating from high school Jennifer decided she would work to become a teacher and earned a teaching diploma after two years of post-secondary education. At the age of thirty, twelve years into her teaching career, Jennifer began to date a male colleague. He seemed to be a wonderful Christian man to her, exactly the type of guy she was hoping to meet and marry. He was an active member of a church and had been involved in missions. Jennifer was in love. "I could stay awake all night just dreaming about him," she told me over dinner one evening.

Despite his seemingly strong Christian values, Jennifer's boyfriend kept pressuring her to have sex. Jennifer resisted his advances, sticking to her commitment to save sex for marriage. On only one occasion she weakened, and became pregnant as a result. When she told her boyfriend about the pregnancy, he thought it was a trap to force him into marriage. He wanted Jennifer to get an abortion, but Jennifer was put off. She "didn't think anyone would want to kill their child." Her boyfriend's pressure to abort made Jennifer feel as though she didn't want to work things through with him. As it turned out she didn't need to try, because he abandoned her and his child. By the time Jennifer was three months pregnant, he had backed out of their relationship. He stayed at their school until the end of the year and came to see the baby twice in a very noncommittal sort of way. Shortly thereafter he moved to another city, then to another country.

Jennifer was left alone to face the consequences of her boyfriend's sexual pressure. She was racked with guilt and shame, feeling she didn't deserve a happy, normal relationship with anyone. She felt she had betrayed her church, her family, her students, and everyone who trusted her. Bearing the increasingly obvious pregnancy alone became strenuous both emotionally and physically, especially with her former boyfriend still around.

Jennifer had a baby girl she named Ella, and cared for her mostly alone. She got six months maternity leave and then was able to have a young cousin live with her to care for Ella while she was teaching. Her home was right beside the school so she was able to come home at lunchtime to see her daughter. When Ella was four years old Jennifer had the opportunity to come to Canada to attend her sister's graduation. She came with an internal agenda to stay, hoping to begin a new life for herself and her daughter. Jennifer loved her job teaching high school students. She was motivated to immigrate mostly because the teacher's pay in Kenya was "miserable". Jennifer strove to get her visitor's visa changed to a student visa and began working at a multicultural center as a program director for women and children. "I didn't expect to find love," she remembers, but she did. A man named Christophe who had recently come from the Congo came to the multicultural center to volunteer and it did not take long for the two of them to hit it off.

About a year and a half after they met Jennifer and Christophe were married. Ella, almost seven years old by this time, was reluctant to accept a man into her life at first as she thought he would take away all of her mother's attention, but within a few months Ella was making statements like, "I think I'm going to marry my Dad." Just three months into their marriage, Jennifer was surprised to discover she was pregnant. Though she was not planning to have a baby anytime soon, it did not take her long to get used to the idea. Jennifer wrote these words in a baby book: "I have a sweet little friend who overturned my world…My little friend was so tiny. Yet she made her presence within me the only thing I could think about during my waking or sleeping hours. Our friendship will last forever. So strongly are we bonded that nothing will ever separate us."

Christophe was a little slower to warm up to the idea of having a baby so soon, but became completely enthralled with their new daughter, Jade, as soon as she was born.

When Jade was just one month old the family made a major move to another city to enable Christophe to attend a nursing college that offered instruction in French. He had been having trouble learning the concepts in English and they felt it would be better for him to take his training in French, which is Congo's official language as a former French territory. Shortly after they moved Christophe discovered the Internet, and become entranced with chat rooms. He began to spend many hours in front of the computer, ignoring his wife and daughters almost completely.

After some time of feeling very lonely in her marriage, Jennifer realized she needed to face the truth—Christophe was having an affair with someone he'd met over the Internet. She remembered a trip she had made to visit her sister in the United States. Christophe had made an excuse to stay home, and was markedly different after her return. Jennifer believes it was while she was away that Christophe physically met the woman he had begun a chat room relationship with and began to have a sexual relationship with her.

Jennifer grieves the loss of her marriage, though she freely admits she mourns the dream of having a happy family more than mourning the man himself. She says she sees now that they began their marriage on a weak foundation, largely motivated by isolation and mutual need. Christophe's recent behavior has caused Jennifer to lose respect for him. When she confronted Christophe about the facts surrounding his unfaithfulness, he was not at all apologetic. He said it was acceptable to have and to cover up an affair because Jennifer had become too busy with schoolwork. He suggested they live together as roommates, support each other through school, and then separate. Jennifer refused. Though it was Christophe who was unfaithful, it was Jennifer who eventually had to move out into her own apartment, making it appear as though the separation was her own initiation. Christophe has done nothing to refute this false assumption but has publicly accused Jennifer of marrying him in order to gain her citizenship.

Jennifer felt Christophe was wanting her to beg and plead with him to end his relationship. She told me she had too much self-respect to do that. Jennifer was quietly sad as she told me these things, but not angry. She has somehow kept herself free from the life-robbing roots of bitterness. Three months after Jennifer moved out with her two girls into a small two-bedroom apartment, the woman Christophe was having an affair with called her to apologize and told her she was not aware that Christophe was married. Some time later Christophe expressed interest in trying to restore their relationship, but Jennifer was not at all convinced that he would make the changes he needed to make.

Jennifer and Christophe are now legally separated and would be divorced if Christophe did not keep doing things to inhibit the divorce from being finalized. Jennifer suspects he is hindering the process because he wants an excuse to keep him from making a commitment to the other woman, with whom he now has a child.

Christophe paid child support very sporadically at first and is now defying court orders to pay support in spite of the fact that he has now graduated and has secured a well-paying job. Meanwhile, Jennifer struggles to support her two daughters and herself all on her own. When Christophe comes to pick Jade up for their official visits, Jade announces cheerfully to Jennifer, "Daddy's here! This is my Dad," as though she is introducing him to Jennifer. It breaks Jennifer's heart because it is a constant reminder that things are not right.

"How did things get so complicated?" she wonders. "But I still hope in God. I know we can let God down—but God won't let us down." Jennifer has courageously decided to pursue a nursing degree, attending classes and doing coursework while her daughters attend school and daycare. She works and studies hard, caring for her daughters in the midst of all her mothering and training responsibilities. "Being a mother has made me less selfish," Jennifer observes. "My life used to be all about me. Then I needed to start living for someone else. It has brought out the tender, gentler, more nurturing person in me. I didn't know I could be so fond of anything."

A new concern has appeared on Jennifer's horizon lately—the probability that Christophe will move far away to be with the woman he had an affair with and their child. Jennifer herself will not miss Christophe but she worries about the long-term effects their father's disappearance will have on her daughters, Jade in particular. Currently Jade sees her Dad once a week and every second weekend. She enjoys spending time with him. Ella often goes as well, but sometimes chooses to stay home with her mother or to be by herself as she is now old enough to be home alone. "It's another transition," Jennifer tells me, or maybe herself, over the phone.

Whatever happens, Jennifer's strength of character and commitment, and especially her remarkable grace and hope will carry both her and her daughters through anything. "I have great hopes for my daughters," Jennifer courageously affirms. "The breakup has been such a setback, but it has not destroyed my hope for them. They are blossoming into successful women. Even when I get very down, and feel life has been so traumatizing, for their sake, I am able to weather many storms."

Chapter 5

Days of Preparation

Journal Entries

May 15th

Realized this morning that having this baby means there will be a whole new person on earth, someone who wouldn't otherwise exist here.

May 17th

Today Daniel asked me out of the blue, "May I have a baby?"

September 11th

Had a dream last night that had many strange elements, as my dreams usually do. I had a baby boy, a third one. He came early and so many other things were going on. I was apart from the boys due to busyness. I forgot to call my parents, and the boys, and hadn't had time to pick a name yet. Maybe this dream is a reflection of me not feeling ready yet, because I don't.

October 9th

Came to realize today that I will be learning a selfless sort of love – a love that gives up pleasure, self-will, health, time, its own body – to give someone else life. In a small way, I will love as Jesus has loved me.

October 15th

I have been forgetful and distracted lately. Today I couldn't find the stroller anywhere, then figured out after awhile that I had left it at the library. I felt a little better about this after I remembered there was no child in it when I brought it there. I used it for hauling my heaps of books back, then forgot to pick up the stroller on the way home because I wasn't burdened by the books.

However, this type of forgetfulness is not an isolated incident. I also paid for groceries but forgot to pick them up, and have twice forgotten to bring my wallet when I took the boys out for breakfast (both times at the same restaurant).

The other day I was out on errands and the mother ahead of me started to depart with her four children in tow, accidentally leaving her charge card behind. I told her, "Don't feel bad. I forgot my groceries the other day."

"I always say, 'At least it wasn't a child'," she replied. I agreed.

We were out somewhere the other day and Tim asked me, rather worriedly, if I was going to forget them.

October 30th

"Hold fast, for I am with you. Stand still, for I am your God. Be quiet before Me, for I have arranged all things for you according to My good will, yes, according to My eternal purposes. For I have purposes and plans and desires which reach far beyond your present view. You see only the immediate situation but My thoughts for you and My planning for you embrace eternity. Yes, you are in My hand. Rest there, and leave all else to Me." [1]

December 1st

A dark morning, and a negative pregnancy test.

December 15th

Wondering this morning when the baby will begin, then read this:

"O My child, it is not appointed to you to know the future, nor to be able to discern beforehand My exact plans. It is enough that we should walk together in love and trust."[2]

Goes with Acts 1:7 rather well: "It is not for you to know the times or dates the Father has set by His own authority."

December 25th

Last Christmas I was wondering what this Christmas would bring. This Christmas I am wondering what next Christmas will bring.

January 16th

Tim's ninth birthday today. He asked for another little brother.

February 2nd

I am in a hotel room in Nashville, done with trying to deny the fact that my bleeding means what it means. I was hoping it was just a little implantation bleeding. After a while, I could deny the evidence no longer and had to face another round of hope and disappointment. "I have good news and bad news," I told Herb on the phone, referring to a hopeful conversation with a publisher, and the dripping disappointment he could probably sense in my voice. After I talked with him and the boys I sat sadly on the hotel room's heater and cried, thinking, *I don't want to go through this again.*

March 10th

Today Daniel told me, "You should have a baby." Then he added emphatically, "ONE baby." This clarifying comment was triggered by a recent visit from Becki and Kelvin's twins, who are now officially into things.

March 16th

Tired tonight. It's almost midnight. I have pretty severe pain in my right ovary again. It aches all the way down my leg when I'm tired sometimes. Just found out a couple of days ago

I will be getting an ultrasound to check for a cyst, which we have to wait two months for. How many months will we have to wait for a baby?

May 7th

"I know you have an idea in your head on how everything should unfold in your life... Because I love you, I need you to give Me back all your plans for today and all your tomorrows.

If you let Me have your day, I can then intervene with something special. My intervention will give you more joy in your journey than all your good intentions. I know all that your heart longs for, and I want to do more for you than you could ever do for yourself. So give Me a chance to change your agenda from ordinary to extraordinary, because that's the kind of life I've destined you to live, My beloved."[3]

May 8th

I called my 93-year-old Oma today for Mother's Day. She told me in her strong Austrian accent, "You should be sankful for dose vonderful boys." She's right. This time of waiting has caused me to become more thankful for the children we've been given, more thankful for the sweet moments we can share together, more appreciative of their little voices, their soft hands and cheeks. I am very definitely blessed. May I never forget it.

Today for our Mother's Day service Cherise sang "*It is Well with My Soul*". She's never sung in church before. This was a deliberate act of faith on her part. Her voice broke after a few lines and the people all joined in to support her even though hardly anyone knows what she's been through— *"When sorrows like sea billows roll; Whatever my lot, Thou has taught me to say, 'It is well, it is well with my soul."*[4] I am sure that song was heard in heaven.

June 17th

Waited over an hour for the doctor this morning. No cyst showed up on the ultrasound. I am not sure if this is good news or not. I would have liked to find something fixable, and an explanation for my pain. Now I will be having exploratory surgery. Didn't think things would come this far. Somehow, I had this thought that having Daniel would have gotten my reproductive system going again. I really wasn't expecting to have to go through infertility again.

July 23rd

Woke early yesterday morning to a pink sky and hoped it was symbolic, but the test was negative—again. Found this morning's devotional to be rather timely:

"Lord, sometimes I am discouraged by the way situations work out – by the way my plans for life fail. My hopes and dreams dissolve into disappointment, and I find myself feeling hopeless. When I'm at that place, help me to trust You more. …I ask You to renew my hope and open my eyes to the spiritual significance of life's disappointments, challenges, and frustrations. I am choosing to believe that You, my Father, know what is best for me, and that You're in control of the tiniest details in my life." [5]

August 16th

Came upstairs after church to the noise of loud cheering. I wondered what the large cluster of people was doing at the back of the church. Upon examination, I found a bunch of guys were racing Becki and Kelvin's twins, who have recently begun to crawl. The men were rooting very loudly, and I was worried about how the babies would feel about this, especially whoever landed up "losing."

"Guys," I admonish the boisterous crowd.

"Oh, it's Auntie Liz," one of the men warns, who I had chastened just the night before for laughing at Lisa's little Jillian when she accidentally hit herself with some sort of stick.

She'd looked hurt to me, wounded that people would laugh at her when she'd hurt herself. The race went on Auntie Liz or no Auntie Liz but at least I was there to feel sorry for little Aiden, a couple of hands behind his brother at the finish line.

August 25th

Spent the entire night in emergency trying to get help for the bronchitis/pneumonia I've been battling. Then we had to leave for our fourteen-hour drive to visit Herb's family. I would have been able to get home and get some sleep if some sort of machine in the lab hadn't been down. They wanted to make sure I wasn't pregnant before giving me the medication. I knew I wasn't, but still hoped for a "shock."

In the bed beside me there was a young woman pregnant for the first time who was twelve weeks along and having chest pain. She was having a difficult pregnancy and sick a lot. I almost broke through the curtain separating us to go and encourage her because the doctor was no help. "It gets worse. You get no sleep after they're born," he told her, between rounds of donuts and coffee. Not exactly what she needed to hear. I prayed for someone to encourage her, and a very nice porter came for her and said some very sweet things.

When I was checking in, the police brought in a woman who'd been beaten by her "partner." She stood at the check-in desk in silence, bruises all over her face, flanked by two officers who completely ignored her. The nurse showed her marginal compassion. She just asked the standard questions, one of which is "Have you been in a hospital for more than 24 hours in the past six months?"

"No," the battered woman replied.

"Didn't you just have a baby?" one officer asked.

"Oh – yeah. A week ago."

Later, she walked around the ward trying to bum cigarettes off of the other patients. The guy beside me was very drunk, and very unreceptive to her request. At times like these, I have a lot of different thoughts churning around inside my mind at the same time. The prevailing one that night was of wondering where the week-old baby was, and wanting to hold its tiny hand, and take it away from the horrific situation it had been born into.

October 1st

Had a dream about two strong lines appearing on a pregnancy test – a thrilling surprise, then when I went back to check the test, the lines had faded.

October 28th

Yesterday I had surgery for the first time in what feels like a long time. I only got three holes this time, a record low. One time when I came out of surgery a nurse said something about having "shrapnel wounds" but it was less complicated this time. Still, the first trip to the bathroom after surgery is always a complicated affair. When you come out of surgery you feel like you've been hit by an airplane. Pathetically, I was actually looking forward to surgery. When the intake nurse asked me if I was feeling nervous about the procedure I told her I was looking forward to a day in bed.

Strangely, the day was rather a big day for women on both sides of the family. Herb's brother's wife Tracy had surgery to remove a softball-sized ovarian cyst, and my brother's wife Carmela had a baby boy, who came out "the emergency exit" as Herb put it. I got the news about our new nephew when my three guys came to pick me up. They made me guess the baby's name, which I wasn't quite up to I guess because I couldn't think of very many boys' names that began with an F. Fletcher Fred Rick was what they were looking for, and I was thrilled that my brother and his wife got a boy to go with their girl, and that my Dad finally got someone named after him. He has been hinting, none too subtly, for his past three grandchildren that Fred or Frederica would be great names.

November 14th

In a rather amusing reflection of the relationship between Pam and I we gave each other chili today. She made some for me for when I was recuperating from surgery, and I made some for her to help out with the extreme busyness of her life right now. We smiled, shrugged, and exchanged margarine containers.

December 31st

Watched "Fiddler on the Roof" last night with a group of friends. I didn't catch all of it due to the fact that we were babysitting the twins for the night, but the words of "Sunrise, Sunset" are still echoing around inside. I was teary last night and lay awake well past midnight crying over how happy I am with Herb, how proud I am of our children, how fast babies grow, how I want another child—not just yet.

When Becki and Kelvin came to pick up Izac and Aiden in the morning, I told her about how many bananas they ate, how many poopie diapers they had, and how they woke up in the night and danced to Bony M Christmas music on the couch with Herb at 2:30 a.m. I say nothing to her of my tears at midnight. She would not understand just yet. Then again, maybe she would.

January 1st

The year is turning—again. I was thinking Herb and I would be 44 and 33 when we had our baby, but I have recently turned 34 and am still not pregnant. It seems that for many of the past New Years, I hope the new year will bring two things, both of which start with a P and neither of which I have much control over: pregnancy and publication.

January 26th

During Moms and Kids Morning this morning Baby Bradley was not happy downstairs without his Mommy so he got to come upstairs and watch a sushi-making workshop. He ate a lot of rice, and got a lot of snuggles from his mother. "I don't call him a mistake," she told us, "He's our surprise." After having a daughter and a son, Charlene and her husband thought they were done having children but were wrong. When Charlene found out she had somehow gotten pregnant, she was nervous to tell her husband. She gave him a card that told him, "Our family is growing by two feet" and he asked her, "Who's this for?"

January 31st

At our women's executive meeting tonight Cherise told us that Theodore has had a change of heart and mind about adopting. They are going to be parents!! This is such a marvelous miracle, filling me with so much joy that I felt like standing up and shouting, "Praise the Lord!" Being reserved by nature I quelled the urge but shouldn't have, because I broke into tears instead. Other people had the same problem.

February 3rd

This morning in church I startled Theodore by rushing up and hugging him when he was trying to hand out bulletins. For me, this is one of those things you realize afterward that you really shouldn't have done, but can't erase. I called Cherise later and apologized and she said very smoothly, "Oh, we didn't mind." I am hoping they were amused, unlike my visiting father-in-law who happened to walk by at just the right moment to witness the assault.

February 14th

Valentine's Day today. A day to love, but isn't that what every day is for? Tim threw up at school today—in the garbage can. He thought he ate too much candy at the Valentine's party, but I think he's actually sick. This afternoon I snuggled and held hands with Daniel for half an hour while he watched a video instead of slipping off to the computer like I'd planned. I don't regret it.

I have been experiencing a new sort of peace lately. It includes a complete yieldedness about this new child, about when, how, and even if he or she comes to us. The unknown isn't really unknown. It is yet to be revealed.

Diane's Story

On the opening page of the article Diane is writing about her road to motherhood she says, "I have always wondered why I was dealt this hand in life. Many people, over the years, have told me they believe we are only challenged in life with what the Lord feels we can handle. Many times I have felt angry when faced with statements such as this but deep down, I know there is some truth behind those words…Sometimes I wished that I didn't have the strength and courage that I possessed…"

Diane was twenty-four years old and just about to be married when she was diagnosed with ovarian cancer. In addition to the physical suffering she endured she was dealt a blow to the heart. After losing the only ovary she was born with during cancer treatment, Diane realized her chances of conceiving and carrying a child were almost impossible. Her only hope to bear a natural child now lay in the possibility of in vitro fertilization using donor eggs. After consulting an in-vitro clinic in another city, Scott and Diane decided the long-shot odds were simply not worth the expense and effort and decided to open an adoption file.

Four years after taking their first steps toward adoption, it looked like Scott and Diane were in luck. A young woman they heard about through a personal contact accepted them as adoptive parents. However, after delivering a baby girl, the birthmother had second thoughts and decided to keep the baby. Scott and Diane never even got to see the child they were sure would become theirs. Their house was full of baby things they could barely stand to look at. A friend came and helped them pack it all away.

After this heart-breaking experience, Scott and Diane decided to pursue the possibility of having Diane's youngest sister be a surrogate for them. While they were away on one of the trips they needed to take to her sister's place, a message was left on their machine from the adoption agency. A fifteen-year-old girl was interested in selecting Scott and Diane as parents in the adoption plan she was making for the baby she would be delivering very soon.

Six days after the call, the teenage girl gave birth to a baby girl and the baby was brought to Scott and Diane's home—for one night. "I knew we were going to get used," Diane sensed at the time. She held the newborn baby like she would hold a niece, keeping herself detached from considering herself the child's mother. She had a strong sense that she shouldn't bond with this child. Sure enough, the adoption agency phoned the next morning. The birthmother had asked for the baby back because her mother and other relatives had pressured her into keeping the baby.

Nine months after this loss, the couple's hopes rose again. Diane's best friend's niece became pregnant. She chose to make an adoption plan for her child, with Scott and Diane identified as parents, and went to their adoption agency to legalize the process. It seemed there wasn't anything that could go wrong this time. However, when the birthmother went to the agency, the agency was obligated by their policies to show other adoptive couples on file. The birthmother was shown sixteen, which she needed to narrow down to four couples, then to two final choices. Scott and Diane and another couple were her finalists. The characteristics of the two couples were almost identical, including the husband's name. Unbelievably, the birthmother chose the other couple because the other woman liked to do crafts. This was a devastating blow to Diane; especially since she herself liked to do crafts but just hadn't happened to mention crafts anywhere on her forms.

Diane decided she could not play the adoption roulette game anymore. She felt like she was on a yo-yo. They began to pursue the possibility of her sister's surrogacy again, and tried to forget about the babies that had come so close to them, yet were so far away. After returning home from another trip to Diane's sister's there was again a message from the adoption agency about a possible placement. They guarded their hearts; not really believing anything would come of it. Scott and Diane did decide to proceed with the adoption, but far more guardedly. Diane tried to be all business. She didn't set anything up for the baby because she couldn't bear to take it all down again. "We have a cradle. He can sleep in there if he comes home," she told herself. Forty-eight hours after giving birth, the twenty-nine year old birthmother did come, accompanied by the agency's social workers, to deliver a baby boy to Scott and Diane, the parents she had selected for her baby. Scott and Diane warmly welcomed the little boy into their home and into their hearts.

Eleven days after dropping off her son, the birthmother came for a visit. The visit appeared to go well, however; just a couple of days later she phoned their home, and Scott and Diane sensed she had changed her mind. Not long afterward, social workers came to take away the baby that had been with Scott and Diane for two whole weeks. The birthmother had decided to take her baby back because she had been fighting with her family and the tension had swayed her toward hanging onto the baby.

After fourteen days of mothering a baby boy, Diane had to hand him back into the hands of the agency, which had to hand him back into the hands of an unstable birthmother. The agency sent all four of their social workers to Scott and Diane's home that day. "They thought they'd have to scrape me off the floor," she stated.

Diane knew the sort of circumstances the innocent baby would be going into, and her heart broke thinking of the life he could have had with them.

So here they were again, unbelievably, with shattered hopes and dreams, and baby things to pack up and put away—again. "What angered me the most is that these women didn't think about us at all. I wanted to scream, 'Do you see what you did to my life?'" Diane felt she'd lost all ability to trust people. She also felt bitter, angry, and defeated. Then she began to feel rejected, like maybe something was wrong with her and Scott. "Why, why is this happening?" she asked herself. The reversal rate for adoptions was one or two out of ten placements. How could this possibly have happened to them four times?

At this point, Scott and Diane both felt defeated. Their families recognized the dangerous emotional space the couple was in and quickly banded together to buy them a week's vacation in the Dominican Republic. The space of time and a place away from their devastating disappointments prevented them from falling into a deep pit of despair. All throughout the years of agonizing waits and losses, the support of family and friends helped to carry Scott and Diane through places they otherwise may have gotten stuck in.

"I do not want this anymore. Don't let me change my mind," Diane told Scott. They mutually agreed to emotionally close the adoption door—but their file was left open at the adoption agency. Seven months later they got a phone call. A twenty-year-old birthmother was due soon. She'd decided to make an adoption plan for her child and her family was supportive. Scott and Diane were understandably hesitant, but couldn't say no to the possibility of getting a baby. Just two days after the initial phone call informing them of the situation, the baby was born, early. Scott and Diane needed to make a difficult decision quickly.

They decided to pursue the adoption but this time, Scott and Diane needed to find a way to protect themselves from another life-shattering disappointment. They told the agency they wanted the baby placed in foster care for the entire twenty-one days in which the birthmother had the legal right to reverse her decision. They simply could not survive another loss. Agonizingly, the twenty-one days had to be doubled into forty-two days because the birthfather went into hiding, thinking he would be held financially responsible for his child. The days of waiting were long and torturous. Diane and Scott didn't set anything up until the night before the baby was to be delivered to them. They refused to so much as see the child until they were granted unalterable custody of her. "Until we saw her she was a name, a dream, a hope. If we saw her, she would be a reality we would have to let go." After forty-two long days, Meredith became a reality.

The birthmother came with the adoption workers to the home she'd chosen for her baby. "Would you like to hold your daughter?" she asked Diane. And then she placed Meredith in Diane's arms. Twelve years after her battle with cancer, Diane became a mother—for good. After all the tears she'd shed throughout the past agonizing years, Diane found herself dry-eyed when she finally took her daughter into her arms. "It felt right—like it was supposed to happen. Now when I cry, I cry tears of happiness."

There were times in her life when Diane wondered if she was even going to live. And then there were times when she wondered if she wanted to live through what she was going through. "I still pinch myself sometimes," she told me as her growing baby crawled around on her floor. "Meredith is such a miracle child to us. It was worth everything."

I hadn't met Diane yet when a friend showed me the poignant letter she'd sent to people who gave them baby gifts, but I cried. And then I did what she told us to:

The hardest thing for us as a couple over the years has been attending functions where everyone seems to have a child. We can finally begin this wonderful journey that most of our friends and family have already been on…parenthood!

We truly have been blessed with a miracle. We are enjoying every moment with her and treasure every smile, every cuddle and every new experience she bestows upon us.

When you receive this letter, please hug and kiss your children, no matter how big and grown-up they are. Let them know that you love them, for they truly are life's greatest treasures.

On Books and Babies

These are two of my favorite things in this world. Books and babies display all of the differences you would expect between paper and flesh, yet they often share a remarkable amount of similarities. Both babies and books can escort you into a whole new world. Both can make you laugh, or cry, or think. Both can upset or uplift you. Both can bring a song into a heart. Books and babies can dramatically change both you and your life. These sorts of powers give evidence to the truth that a book is more than paper, and a baby is more than flesh.

When a child comes into our lives, our world is automatically enlarged without any effort or intent on the child's part. The child changes us just by existing. When we take a child into our hearts we are changed—not just by the child but by our love for the child. Some books can also change us if we take them into our hearts, without any effort on the book's part. With children as well as with books—there is an invisible author at work.

Sometimes it seems there are two sorts of people when it comes to books and babies—those who treasure them and those who don't. Some see children as blessings, some see them as burdens. Some see books as boring, some as see them enlightening. The blue glare of the television has so permeated culture that shadows rarely darken pages anymore but there are still survivors of technological tyranny who light up their lives with books. Since you're reading this chapter, which is almost at the end of a book, you are probably a survivor and already know about the potential power between the covers of a book. If you are a mother you most certainly already know about the life-changing potential within a child. I cannot think of much I could say to a reading mother about reading books or raising babies that she doesn't already know, so perhaps I will write a little about writing.

If you've ever tried to write a book you'll know that a book you call your own is an entirely different matter than a book you buy or borrow, in the same sort of way that a baby you call your own is entirely different to you from a baby you baby-sit or admire in the mall. A baby or a book that isn't yours may interest you, delight you, or frustrate you, but never to the same degree as one that is yours. You may notice and may even be bothered by faults in a book or a child that is not yours to deal with, but you are far more detached than with your own child or book because you know that you do not need to try to fix those faults. Someone else's book or someone else's child may bless you, inspire you, discourage you, enrage you, run through your mind, or teach you something, but never as deeply as your own.

Both books and babies need far more work, and produce far more fascination, than you bargained for. Both induce a fiercely protective attitude. A writer has a strange sort of tendency to see their work as their child, becoming extremely defensive and protective at any hint of imperfection. Editors have their own terms for overprotective authors but I am not sure how many of them are publishable. Editors, you see, are not in love with an author's child like the author is. Love does have a tendency to be blind toward faults, which is not always a bad thing.

I have been going to a few writers' conferences lately, supposedly to boost my credibility and professionalism. I find it strange that publishers think you're serious about your writing if you go to a conference. In my opinion conferences are a big treat, providing both vacation and inspiration. Personally, I think if publishers really want to know if you're serious they should ask how many times you've been rejected and kept trying, or maybe ask for a picture of you wrestling with your printer at two o'clock in the morning.

At any rate, conferences can be valuable for getting some glimpses of what's actually going on in the publishing world. Writers often go to conferences not so much to learn things as to be around people like them; people who can understand and maybe even respect them, people who can comprehend why they do the sorts of things non-writers consider boring or just plain strange.

Authors tend to isolate themselves a little, for more than one reason. They tend to be quieter personalities of people to begin with. They also need space in which to develop ideas. And, in order to actually get anything written, they need to set themselves apart from televisions, telephones, and endless errands. Not everyone can relate to these needs, or even understand them. I told Herb about the journalist who was writing in New York and didn't know about the twin towers going down until he finally answered his incessantly ringing telephones. That seemed to help Herb accept the fact that I don't always answer a ringing telephone. Plus, after fifteen years, I am catching on to the fact that I shouldn't always need Herb to understand me.

Last winter I went to Nashville to experience one of the industry's trade shows. One of my friends expressed excitement about this trip when she thought I was going to record a CD (she does not know me too well yet). She was quite let down to hear it was actually about books. Nashville was not nearly as warm as Florida, but nice enough for a Canadian who desperately needed to thaw out. I walked around parking lots with my little wheeled backpack just to soak in the February sun that felt like a well-advanced spring to me. On one of my parking lot excursions I visited a steakhouse that perhaps typifies Nashville. The sign on the outside offered diners a ten percent discount if they showed a church bulletin on Sundays. Inside, the waitresses wore T-shirts that asked, "24 hours in a day. 24 beers in a case. Coincidence?"

Writing-related trips can be both constructive and destructive. You can get both inspired and overwhelmed. You can find yourself thinking, "What could I possibly add to all this?" and "If this book can get published then certainly my book should be able to" within a couple of minutes while walking an exhibit floor, or browsing in a bookstore. You can often get very conflicting opinions and advice about your work. You can feel very small very quickly if you compare and compete the way you're encouraged to. You can find out someone else is writing what you're writing. Not to mention that you are quite liable to meet someone who's published fifty-eight "award-winning" books in the same amount of time it's taken you to hammer out an outline.

I think most people get into writing the same way most people get into parenting—pretty idealistically. Personally, I had absolutely no idea how difficult it would be to write a whole book let alone get it published. I did not know that publishing companies receive thousands of submissions every year and publish only a handful. I did not know I would be looked upon as more of a nuisance than anything, or that I would have to fight so hard to break through publishing barriers, or jump through so many hoops to even begin to be noticed. I did not know that publishing houses have stacks and drawers full of what they call "slush" from people like me. And by the time I found these things out, it was too late. I had gone too far. Or maybe I should I say I was too far gone.

If someone is interested in being famous or making money, I would recommend they try anything other than writing to reach those goals. If someone is interested in being stripped of all self-interest and self-centeredness, I would recommend writing and re-writing and re-writing a book or two. Trying to get a book published is an excellent endeavor to embark upon in order to get rid of selfish motivations, especially after the realization dawns that it is pretty well impossible to get either rich or famous by doing so. I have left both fame and fortune behind now and have come to the point of knowing that my writing was never meant to be about my own glory or benefit.

If, on the inside of me, this is really true—that my writing is not about me and not for my own glory, then I really don't need to compare my work or my self with anyone or anything else. I really shouldn't be bothered by rejections, and I absolutely must refuse to play against authors who are supposed to be teammates. If I say my work is not about me, then it can't be about me. Unlike the restaurant in Nashville, I want what my sign says on the outside to match what things look like on the inside.

For the first while after I started writing, I didn't tell anybody. That was smart of me and sometimes I wish I'd kept my mouth shut longer. I started to talk about the book I was working on (currently languishing in someone's slush pile) when I thought I was nearing the end of the road, only to find out it was more like the beginning. "How's the book coming?" people will often ask me.

"Slowly but surely," I usually respond. (More often than not, the "surely" part is more hopeful than factual.)

"Will it be a long book?" one sweet woman queried very politely.

Sometimes I try to figure out why writing a book takes so long for so many people, myself in particular. I map out the months that my work has been neglected and then look for some sort of explanation—moving, surgery, pneumonia, traveling, teaching, other projects. As always, misery loves company so I felt much relief upon learning that *Moby Dick* took 33 years to write. (I have decided not to talk or even think about one of my writing instructors who has recently published his 100th book.) In theory, a person could write a page a day and produce a fairly complete manuscript in a year. This is strictly a theory, which does not take into account all the draftiness and difficulties that an average writer runs into. Nor does it display awareness of the fact that children, husbands, churches, friends, families, and houses sometimes literally scream for attention while a computer is easy to ignore, and difficult to stay at.

Babies are loud. While not everyone is moved enough by their cries to answer them, everyone can at least hear them. Books are loud too, but only to the person they're living inside. They seem to be silent to everyone except those who are destined to bring them forth. Books are heavy burdens to bear for it sometimes seems they are never silent, weighing on you and calling for you even when you set them down, perhaps especially then. Plus, you cannot get a book babysitter. Someone might toss them a cracker now and then, but they are yours alone and there is no getting around it.

Sickness and stretch marks aside, I believe bearing books has been harder on me than bearing babies has. Babies sleep, at least in snatches, but books are restless and never seem to sleep, spinning circles around inside your head, creating a sort of dizzy effect. Over the years, I have developed a twenty-second delay between hearing something and responding to it, kind of like a radio station. I know my mental dizziness can usually be attributed more to my sleep deficit accrued over many years of late night writing shifts than to really profound thoughts swirling around in my head, but perhaps if I try to look thoughtful people will think I'm more profound than dazed. Then again, maybe they won't, if one friend's recent observation is any indication. "You look either stoned or really tired," she told me one morning. Given those two options, I told her I was tired. I probably was anyway.

Tim and I have been scanning some books by a woman named May Sarton. I got quite a number of her books out of the library for the purposes of studying how she writes since that is what one is supposed to do—study works in the same genre as what one is writing. To reveal exactly how educated I am about this genre, I had never heard of this well-known author until I read a mention of her in a writing manual. She published over forty books. Most of these were poetry or fiction but she also has written rather a number of reflective journals, which is what I stocked up on.

I started off reading *At Seventy* and was both annoyed and amused at first. I was slightly annoyed that something as boring as an elderly woman's daily comments, many of which centered around her cats and gardens, would be well-published while my far-more-interesting-according-to-me manuscripts are still languishing in drawers. This is not a new sort of sentiment for me. I used to get upset every time I walked into a bookstore and saw titles like *The Secret Life of Lobsters*, *Toilets of the World*, or *Rhubarb Recipes* published and flourishing while I couldn't get anybody to even read my work. I guess I am getting so used to this sensation that I moved onto amusement fairly quickly.

I was amused at entries recording things like Sarton's surprise at being bitten by a black fly or her happiness at someone bringing over a hundred and fifty pounds of sunflower seeds. Since I thought Tim would get a kick out of them too I started reading snatches of the journal out loud and it became our entertainment for a while. "This is better than *Calvin and Hobbes*," he commented once. *At Seventy* kept us amused for some time, but *At Eighty-Two* wasn't so funny. Somehow, knowing this was Miss Sarton's last year of life sobered us up as did the picture of her on the back of the book, walking in her garden, grey and stooped with age and sickness. On Christmas Day that year she wrote, "I have a strong feeling that this is the last Christmas. There is something of a farewell now in everything I do—writing Christmas cards, will I ever be able to do it another year?"[6]

Now that I have read more of Sarton's work (even some poetry though I am not really a poetry person) I have a real respect for her and her work, and a sort of sorrow over her suffering though it occurred over a decade ago. The books she produced throughout her lifetime were her children, her lasting legacy, which makes me think of a piece of writing advice I read some time ago—we must treat our books as though they are all we will leave behind in the world.

I have begun to really treasure a new friendship with a couple that lives up our street, Duncan and Brenda. They are nice people in general, and they are also both writers so I know they can understand things about me that other people can't. They can probably recognize and empathize with my "stoned" look. They can relate to the rejections, the distractions, the obsessions, the habits, and the interests that tend to characterize writers. I know they would understand why I don't always pick up the phone, and I strongly suspect they don't either.

Duncan has sort of fascinated Tim ever since Tim's class went on a field trip to the library where Duncan was a writer-in-residence for the year. He told the kids that one of the reasons he likes being a writer is that he doesn't have to comb his hair every morning. He has also made some sort of reference to being hit by lightning when he was over for coffee once, which I still need to get the exact facts on as Herb thinks Duncan was actually being serious. Tim's interest in Duncan increased when Brenda told us about how she had to drop Duncan off to sleep in a coyote-filled desert overnight so he could more accurately describe what he was going to have one of his characters do. (This is one of the reasons I choose to write non-fiction.)

Brenda is also a fiction writer and her first novel will be coming out in a few months, shortly after her second baby is also due to come out. As book contracts are signed far in advance of release dates and tend to be rather inflexible, Brenda had no way of knowing or of changing the fact that she will be delivering both a baby and a book within weeks of each other. I have no idea, and I sense she doesn't either, how she will manage these two massively monumental births. One thing I am sure of. It will be a stretching experience.

Both the books and the babies that we bear stretch us. Both enrich us. Both wriggle into our hearts and stay there—for life. Neither can thrive without our attention. Both will wither and die if left unattended. A book, thankfully, can sit on a shelf or in a drawer and be ignored for many years and still thrive. A baby cannot. Books age well. They do not change if you turn your back on them. They will not go out unless you send them out. They will not grow up and leave without your really noticing their impending departure. But the same cannot be said for babies. They grow rapidly up and away, whether you are prepared to launch them or not.

I have a couple of books somewhere around here, sleeping. I have tucked them away for now. When I am older and wiser I will look for them again, and there they will be—unchanged. I have a couple of boys around here, clattering about. I tuck them away sometimes to sleep but I never need to look for them. They always bound up the stairs to look for me, a little bigger each morning. May they find me each morning, a little older and a little wiser with each passing day.

Barb's Story

"So when are you due?" I ask Barb as we sit together on a couch in my living room with cups of tea after dinner. Barb's cup is regularly endangered by the flailing legs or arms of a little daughter who wants to be near Mommy. All I can hear of her answer is "seventh." Her quiet voice is drowned out by the clamor created by our five children and two husbands.

"Seventh?" I ask.

"May seventh," she tells me again. "We'll have four kids four and under."

If there's anyone who can handle this, it's Barb. She has serenity and stamina that, humanly speaking, are inexplicable. I have always been a little puzzled by Barb's immense patience and joy in her mothering since her childhood and teen years were not ones that would tend to result in a calm, secure, and positive sort of woman—the sort of woman Barb has chosen to become.

Barb's parents divorced when she was just three years old. She lived with her father for a few years following the divorce because her mother was an alcoholic and couldn't take care of Barb or her older brother, who went to live with his grandparents on a reservation. When Barb was five or six years old her mother got cleaned up, and Barb was able to live with her for a number of years until her mother's new boyfriend began to sexually abuse Barb when she was about eleven years old. This went on for a few months until one of Barb's aunts picked up on the clues and reported the situation. Barb was placed in foster care for a couple of weeks and then got moved back with her father. She was shocked to find out that he had remarried, had a six-year-old stepson and was expecting another daughter with his new wife.

Barb went to three different schools that year. She lived with her father and his new family for about a year, until a family feud erupted in the small northern community they were living in and the family moved into the city. Barb was accepted fairly well by her father's new wife and enjoyed her little stepsister, but it was not long until she experienced yet another upheaval in her young life. When she was just seventeen, her father and stepmother decided to move far away without communicating their plans to Barb.

Barb ended up staying behind. She stayed with a friend's family for a while. After a few months, another friend's aunt and uncle began to care for Barb and took her in as their own daughter while she finished her last year of high school. After she turned eighteen they were able to legally adopt her. Barb's adoptive parents introduced her to Christ and provided a safe place for her to live, but her adoptive mother struggled with some emotional problems. As a result of the inconsistencies caused by her adoptive mother's depression and instability, Barb never felt completely emotionally safe in their home. She started going to church with her new parents "pretty half-heartedly".

After graduating from high school Barb went to university, and then to Bible College. Barb first met John when they began carpooling to college together. John is an outgoing, cheerful sort of guy, and at first Barb found him "obnoxious" and didn't know what to make of his openness. John's honesty and enthusiasm soon won her over and they became best friends. After three years of being best friends, they got married when Barb was twenty-two and John was twenty-four.

A little more than two years after being married, John and Barb were excited to find out they were going to have a baby. As first-time parents, they also felt a little nervous, not knowing exactly what was ahead of them. Five weeks before the baby was due, Barb's water broke with a pop. "What was that?" she wondered, "What do I do now?" Having the baby early was everything Barb didn't want. She didn't feel at all ready. She was still working, and had a lot of getting ready to do. She hadn't even begun to pack anything for the hospital. John ran around their tiny apartment, wildly flinging clothes around looking for things to pack. Barb, characteristically calmer, found the things he was looking for and they headed to the hospital. Since they got sent home again they got a little extra time but it was not long before the baby was definitely heading out. Even though she was born more than a month early, Rebecca was almost seven pounds at birth and is still in good health, apart from having fairly serious asthma due to underdeveloped lungs.

Barb was delighted with her new baby, and with her new role as a mother. However, she soon received quite a shock shortly into her mothering career when Rebecca was just seven months old. She discovered she was pregnant again. They had been sort of letting nature take its course, not thinking anything would happen anytime soon since Rebecca's conception had taken a number of months to occur. They never expected to have another baby so quickly. Just sixteen months after having Rebecca, Barb gave birth to a second daughter, Jaime. Barb was exhausted after having Jaime and did not feel emotionally prepared to parent her. At just over a year old, Rebecca was still very needy, and very heavy to carry. They didn't have a name ready for Jaime and had to hastily pick one after she was born. It took six months before Barb felt like she'd developed any sort of bond with her second baby.

Almost incredibly, when Jaime was nine months old, Barb suspected she was pregnant again and was "a complete basket case." She felt mortified and became very afraid of what everybody was going to think. John and Barb had gotten "a lot of flack" over having Jaime, and she dreaded people's re-action to another pregnancy. Things were very tight financially for them at that point. Even to buy a seven dollar pregnancy test was a concern, but Barb found she couldn't wait for their next paycheck. She needed to know one way or another. When the test turned positive she thought to herself, "Now I know, let's deal with it." She remembered what she had gone through with Jaime and promised herself things would be different this time. She made herself talk about her feelings with John and it didn't take long for her to accept the baby with her whole heart. She was able to enjoy her pregnancy and newborn days. Barb quickly fell in love with their third daughter, Amber, born just eighteen months after Jaime.

After Amber was born, Barb began to feel a lot of guilt about her earlier relationship with Jaime. She felt she didn't bond or care for Jaime the way she should have when she was a baby. A very defining moment in Barb's mothering was when she was telling John about how guilty she felt and he suggested that she go and apologize to Jaime and tell her she loved her. Barb went to where little Jaime was sleeping in her crib, laid her hand on her back and apologized to her, tearfully telling her she loved her very much. After that night Barb felt like she finally completely accepted and loved Jaime. Something changed in their relationship after that encounter, even though Jaime slept through it.

Barb works more than a full day as a Mommy. She also works as the caretaker of their apartment block. Just to think about her life can be exhausting for me. For a while, we both dropped off our kids at preschool at around the same time, and I watched in amazement as Barb calmly corralled her three children and bulging belly up and down the stairs, in and out of the bathroom, on and off with coats. One morning Jaime had thrown up all over herself twice in the car and Barb had to clean her up with Kleenex and take her back home. Several other times, one or the other of them were almost completely covered in chicken pox scabs. While the two older girls are at pre-school, Barb takes toddler Amber in tow and they sweep and vacuum their apartment building.

Within a few months, John and Barb will be moving to another city to become involved in a new church being begun there. They'll put all their worldly possessions and three small children in a U-Haul truck and take a very long one-way trip shortly before their fourth baby is born. "I guess I have an ability to take on life like it's an adventure," Barb says, referring to the attitude she's taken on about having her children so close together. "I try to have a sense of humor and have just grown to ignore people's comments. We didn't necessarily intend on having our children so close together, but we're choosing to focus on the positive things about having them close in age. People say things to us but we say, 'We're happy. We're glad to have our children. We love them.' And we can say it with a smile on our face because we mean it."

Barb is honest about the challenges she faces, but never whiny. When I asked her what she finds hard about being a mother she said, "Hard? Where to begin?" She can get very frustrated when the girls just can't seem to get along. There are times Barb is surrounded by screaming, fighting, and constant demands; and sometimes feels she yells too much. At times, Barb finds herself facing long days of caring for her children on just five hours of sleep. She is simply overwhelmed sometimes at how trying they are on her patience and she often feels like she doesn't have enough time for all of them. Barb remembers asking God to help her develop patience a number of years ago—and wonders if her three children under three was an answer to that prayer.

"I see how much trust they put in me," Barb said. "Their perception is so pure, so innocent, so open and honest." Barb and John delight in watching their girls learn and develop. They feel that the inescapable responsibilities of parenthood have caused them to grow up a lot. They've found out what parenthood really takes—everything, in some ways. In having their children, they've made unspoken promises and they follow through on them whether they feel like meeting a need or not.

Barb has gone through a couple of bouts with depression, one as a young teenager, and another around the time she turned twenty. Miraculously, she did not suffer from any post-partum depression after the births of any of her babies and has been largely free from any symptoms of depression throughout her mothering career despite the demands on her body and emotions. Barb says she has learned to lean on God's strength to carry her through, and feels His presence with her throughout her day, helping her remain calm when she feels like blowing up. Sometimes she feels like there is a constant hand on her shoulder reminding her of things like, *It's only milk* when the milk gets spilled—again.

One day Rebecca told me she has a baby brother in heaven. I hadn't known about this and asked Barb about it when we were alone. She told me she had recently been pregnant with a very much-wanted baby (John and Barb always planned to have four children). When the pregnancy was six weeks along, she began to spot one night. Barb was worried and upset but lay in bed and said to God, "I know this baby is Yours. I give this baby to You." At that moment, she sensed heavenly hands come and gently take the baby from her. She had a quiet sort of peace realizing that it was time for the baby to go, that it was not meant to be with them. The next day she began to bleed heavily and did lots of crying that morning before going to the hospital as she was advised to. After both Barb and John went through a grieving process for the baby they would never have and hold, they came to understand that even though their baby lived only a short while, it had a definite purpose in their lives.

Shortly after the miscarriage, Barb became pregnant again but didn't become aware of the pregnancy for a couple of months since she was expecting her cycle to be irregular for a while. Not long after she realized she was pregnant and arranged for medical care, both Barb and her midwife began to suspect she was carrying twins. "Actually, we were quite excited," she told me. For a couple of months they prepared themselves for a double addition to their rapidly-growing family. When an ultrasound revealed she was carrying just one child, Barb and John were a little disappointed, evidence of their truly welcoming hearts.

It won't be long now until their fourth child will be born—less than five years after their first. As Barb calmly protects her teacup and her bulging belly from Jaime's flailing appendages, I admire her unassuming loveliness—both inside and out. She has been either pregnant or holding a baby (usually both, actually) for so long that an interior or exterior infant has become an accessory for her, accentuating her dark earth mother look.

We sat with John and Barb at a Valentine's dinner a child or two ago and they got called up to be participants in "The Newlywed Game". One of the questions John got asked was, "What is your wife's dream job?" I found it rather touching when, typical of many young mothers, Barb didn't know how to answer that question when she was asked it. But John had been able to identify exactly what Barb would be perfect for—being a midwife. She is calm, cool, and collected—just the type of person you would want around to keep you company when you were giving birth. For the time being, though, Barb has her hands, her days, and her heart full being a mother. Like every mother, she is perfect for her children.

Relief and Grief

Journal Entries

February 15th

For many of the months that we have been "trying" (strange phrase, but I can't think of a better one), the end of a cycle brings both relief and grief. Sometimes the grief has been strong, eclipsing relief almost completely, but often the relief has been stronger than the grief.

I am busy. I am often tired. I am happy as I am. I am a little conflicted.

February 17th

I have been thinking of giving up on the idea of another birth child. There would still be grief in doing so, but there would also be relief. I would be giving up a lot of hardships, but a lot of pleasures, too. And I'm not totally sure that giving up would be the right thing to do.

February 18th

Went over to some new friends' house tonight for supper. We are coming into the stage where we gain friends through our kids' friends. Sam and Tim are in the same grade at school. Sam has a little sister Lauren who their parents adopted from China when she was nine months old. She is quite precious and this fact is not lost on Herb.

I'm really starting to feel like adopting, but several motivations are still selfish, sparing myself suffering being one of them.

February 19th

Daniel has now caught whatever it was that caused Tim to throw up in the garbage can during his Valentine's party. He threw up three times this morning, once in the produce section in the grocery story. Thank heavens for plastic fruit bags.

March 12th

Today in church we had the twins sitting with us for a while. Naturally, between Tim and Daniel, and Aiden and Izak, things got pretty wiggly sometimes. Becki was sitting behind us and whispered to me, "Don't you wish you had four kids?" I made a face that indicated I didn't but truth be told, I would actually like to have four kids. I am just not sure how to have them, or where to put them.

March 21st

Tonight when I came in after being out for quite awhile I went into the boys' room and found Tim awake and quite happy to see me. "Hi, Mom!" he chirped. I am not sure what things will be like when he is a teenager, but for now it is him who waits up for me. Once when he was four years old I came into his room at ten minutes before midnight—and he was awake, waiting to see me before he fell asleep.

March 26th

One of the reasons I love going on trips is meeting people. One of the life-touching people I met on this trip to a women's conference is Thomasena, a beautiful African-American woman pregnant with her seventh child. We sat at the same table for lunch one day, connecting deeply in a brief amount of time, as women often do. Later she came to sit by me before one of the sessions. "I have to rub on this woman a bit," she told bystanders, "She wants a baby." She set herself down beside me and put a warm hand on my back. I hope she does rub off on me, not just the pregnancy part, but the patience part. Though I have never watched Thomasena with her six children, I can sense that she is full of peace and her children bring her great joy.

Being in a southern state heightens my desire to adopt an African-American baby girl. This has been on my mind for some time now. Out of all the concerns and considerations involved in this one of my most ridiculous has been worrying about how I would take care of her hair. Black hair is complicated, say my African and Barbados friends. I am an uncomplicated person when it comes to hair. We cut our boys' hair so short that we never have to bother even combing it. (Hopefully this will not incline them toward being writers when they grow up.) When I told Thomasena that we've been thinking of adopting a little girl she said to me, "Hair blessings on you," even though I hadn't said a word about my hair worries.

In the airport on the way home I got my period. Again.

April 1st

For once, Tim didn't get heavily into April Fool's Day, though I think he may have pulled something on my Dad. He usually tries to convince him there are twin or triplet calves out in the barn. We are out at my parents' farm for the boys' spring break.

Visited my Oma this afternoon at her apartment. Herb told me when we were alone that he thought this trip would be the last time we would see her.

April 12th

Oma died last night. She was 93 years old. It was time, but that does not change the fact that we will never see her here again. The last time we visited her she was fairly disoriented and had lost almost all of her ability to speak English. For a number of years she'd been lapsing into German more often than not and wondering why people couldn't understand her. (Except when she was in Austria visiting German-speaking relatives. Then, for some strange reason, she mostly spoke her heavily-accented English.)

My sister-in-law had called earlier in the evening to let us know Oma had been taken into the hospital and wasn't doing well. I was out at the time but Herb prepared the boys by saying that he thought Oma might go to heaven soon. She did pass away that night and in the morning I had to tell them Oma was gone. Daniel took the news seriously and quietly. He is too young to really comprehend death, let alone grieve deeply, but Tim knew what this meant. I held him on my lap in the early morning light and let him cry as long as he wanted without saying anything to him. I don't know what he was thinking as he cried. I didn't think I should ask.

I decided to keep him home from school and spend the day with him even though I had a lot of my own things I needed to work through. I took him for a bike ride after some quiet time at home, then out to a café. He had hot chocolate with a lot of marshmallows and whipped cream. I had tea. We didn't have much to say so we didn't say much. Every once in a while, he would seem to think some sort of deep thought and look up at me. Even as the moments passed, I sensed they were eternal.

April 29th

Because my aunt who works as a tour guide had a trip booked for right after her mother died and couldn't get out of the commitment, we had to postpone Oma's funeral until today. Her son picked her up from the airport and they came right away to our hometown, a six-hour drive from the airport.

My aunt and I went to the apartment in the morning to try and sort through things. As she showed me the dishes she'd set aside for my parents she started to cry. "All I can see is her crippled hands," she said, and then I started to cry too because that's exactly what I kept seeing. "I hope she knows we loved her. She worked so hard all her life and I don't know if she enjoyed it."

"She knows you loved her," I say to her, "and she loved you, too. She didn't always say that, but she did." I am not sure if my Oma ever did say to her three children that she loved them. She did though.

It was raining and miserable the day of the funeral. "This is how funerals always look in the movies," Tim said on our way from the church to the graveside, and then added sadly, "Except now I know how it feels."

May 12th

My parents came in today for the Mother's Day week-end. I thought it would be good for them to be here instead of at home. They brought in Oma's embroidery, Austrian dolls, and dining room set; and the old wind-up music box that so fascinated me as a child. Someday I will have a chance to grieve for my Oma, for never hearing her unique voice again or watching her squeeze the children too tightly; for the memories of her braiding my hair too tight, making me eat too much, teaching me how to clean chickens, and make jam. The day she killed a wounded young bear with a shovel. Someday I will sit and cry. Maybe right now.

May 14th

Mother's Day today. "I couldn't help think of my mother today," Dad said after church.

"Mothers are important," I said, not knowing what else to say. I don't think this will go down as my most brilliant response ever.

May 15th

Found out Barb and Jon had their baby just before Mother's Day—a fourth little girl they named Annabelle Hope.

May 19th

I went to a warm water pool today to try to get my back muscles to mellow out. There was a touching group of five women there, presumably for a Mother's Day treat—one very elderly grandmother, two mothers, and two daughters. They were so sweet to the grandmother that it made me teary. I am emotional today even though, hormonally speaking, I shouldn't be anymore. Am I in denial about not minding not getting pregnant?

As one of the daughters was bringing her grandmother a juice one of the mothers noticed a navel ring. I was waiting for a negative reaction but all the mother (or aunt or whatever) said was, "Does it hurt?"

The other mother said, "It looks nice."

May 30th

Daniel is in soccer for the first time this year. Watching him on the sunny field wearing his little blue hat struck a chord in me today. I got to watch him score his first goal but what was really moving for me was just seeing him so alive and healthy. It was a reminder of how happy I am that he is still with us, and how I must not take this, or any, child for granted.

June 10th

Our neighbors Duncan and Brenda brought their little boy Sebastian to watch Daniel's soccer game tonight. Brenda is quite elegantly pregnant now. We talked about miscellaneous writing projects and Brenda expressed her anxiety over how she will be able to launch her novel while managing Sebastian, and having a very new baby. Sebastian will only be twenty-two months when the baby arrives.

June 24th

Went camping this weekend with a few families from church, our first time tenting since we've had Daniel. I awoke in the morning to the sound of a number of babies crying in chorus, which I didn't really mind because none of them were mine to worry about. I could just lie in my warm bed and listen to them. Sitting on someone's picnic table later while drinking some of their coffee I mentioned the fact that it is nice not to have to deal with babies anymore, a deceptive sort of comment on my part. “Yeah, that’s what we thought, too,” one father comments who was surprised with a son after two daughters. “Brigitte came into the bedroom and told me she was late. I didn’t know what for.”

July 20th

Got a call from Cherise today asking if she can borrow our crib. They have been selected as parents for two beautiful little boys, 6 and 2 years old.

July 28th

Spending a couple of days at my parents cabin with just my two boys—a very special time. If I had a baby when I’d wanted to, we wouldn’t be able to do this. Started feeling for the first time today that maybe I don’t want any more children. It would certainly be easier.

August 3rd

Today is Theodore and Cherise’s first official day as parents. Really, they have already been with the children quite a lot—the transition from the foster home was rather rapid. Doubtless this abrupt change is challenging, and there are probably more challenges ahead. Cherise’s amazing grace, perseverance, and faithfulness can handle them all.

August 5th

Had to drive through downtown in the dark on the way home from dropping off a friend. Driving through downtown is always difficult for me, not because of the traffic but because of the things I see. This time I saw an old woman digging in a garbage can for food—is she anyone’s mother? A few blocks later I saw a young woman biking to go work the streets dressed in black fishnet stockings. She had a baby seat on the back of her bike.

August 8th

Feeling today that the desire for another child is almost gone. But I don't want it to be gone for the wrong reasons.

August 22nd

Some time ago my mother-in-law gave me a candleholder with an angel on it. According to the writing at the bottom, she is the "Angel of Courage". When I realized the angel looks a lot like me I began to develop an affinity for it. I've been lighting it every once in a while to help me prepare for the challenges involved in bearing and caring for another child. Sometime before my surgery last fall I moved it or packed it away to make room for Christmas decorations, and now I have no idea where it could be. I am trying not to make the obvious connection—I have lost my courage. But that's kind of how I'm feeling right now.

September 3rd

Read to Daniel on my lap today. As he sat with me all small and soft I thought about his going to school soon. Somehow, it is no longer socially acceptable to feel sad at a child's starting school. Mothers who miss their children are made to feel like they are not emotionally healthy. But I won't deny having some sadness, some deeply poignant moments, maybe even some grief.

You see, I know what this means now. Things won't ever be the same for us again. Sure, I'll be happy to have three hours every morning to work. Sure it'll be a relief to see the school bus drive off some mornings. But I'll miss him, too, my baby, who is now no longer a baby at all.

Relief and grief. They are almost opposites, but these two states are perfectly able to co-exist within a mother's heart, over more than one situation.

Angie's Story

Angie was thrilled to find out she was pregnant after just over a year of marriage, especially after being diagnosed with endometriosis several years before she and Cory were married. Though she loved her job working as a legal secretary, she had always wanted to be a mom. Angie thoroughly enjoyed her pregnancy and delighted at feeling the baby's first kick. At the beginning of her pregnancy, Angie experienced cramping and was terrified that she was losing the baby, but the pregnancy did continue and Angie was able to carry the baby to term.

After going six days past her due date, Angie was anxious to see her baby so when an opportunity came up for her to be induced at eleven o'clock at night, she took it. Labor was intense and didn't progress the way everyone wanted it to. After some time, the baby's heartbeat began to drop. When medical staff lost the heartbeat, a decision was made to perform an emergency Caesarean using an epidural line in Angie's back, which enabled her to be conscious for her baby's delivery. Baby Mackenzie was delivered safely.

Motherhood took some adjustments at first. Angie was used to eating and sleeping whenever she wanted to, and found the needs of her newborn pretty overwhelming. She would find herself thinking, "I just sat down," or "All I want to do is eat.", but Angie's positive attitude toward life helped her adjust and recover quickly. When

Mackenzie was seven months old, Angie went back to work and missed her baby girl terribly. She forced herself to keep working until she got pregnant again seven months later and had her second child, a baby boy they named Ethan.

Ethan was a bright, cheerful baby and apart from having chronic ear infections, he seemed perfectly healthy until one summer day shortly after his second birthday when Angie was bathing him and he kept telling her, "Owie tummy, Mommy." The family had all been sick with the stomach flu, so Angie assumed his discomfort was related to that until she felt his stomach and found a hard lump. She thought it might be something that should be looked at and phoned for a doctor's appointment the next day. Cory took Ethan in for his appointment since Angie was running a home daycare at the time.

When the pediatrician felt Ethan's stomach he became immediately alarmed. He told Cory it was very serious, and asked him where he was parked. The doctor arranged for an emergency ultrasound but wouldn't tell Cory what he thought might be the problem. Cory phoned Angie on his way home, crying, and told her she needed to get her sister to come and look after the kids. When Cory got back home, he didn't come in the house. Angie went out to him and found him almost hysterical. They took Ethan to his ultrasound appointment at the children's hospital and were informed that he had a large mass. "I guess I was naïve," Angie told me. She was thinking, "Well, if it's a mass, then they'll just remove it."

By this time, both sets of grandparents had arrived at the hospital and a number of doctors came to talk to the family. When the last two doctors arrived, they introduced themselves as doctors from the cancer unit. That's when Angie began to realize the severity of what was going on. The ultrasound alone could not determine whether or not the mass was cancerous, nor whether the mass was outside or inside of Ethan's liver, but the doctors told Angie and Cory that the situation was probably very serious.

This happened on a Friday and throughout the weekend Angie was in a state of shocked denial, thinking, "If it is cancer, it'll come out. They'll just take it out." She couldn't yet comprehend that her little boy could have something she couldn't fix. "We're just going to make it better," she told herself. On Tuesday, Ethan underwent a procedure in which he was sedated and dye was shot into his abdomen, a horrifying procedure for a parent to watch. The next morning, they went in to get the results of the test, and that was when the gravity of the situation really sunk in for Angie.

Cory and Angie were told their little boy had a large mass inside his liver which had almost completely consumed the right lobe, spread into the left lobe, and metastisized into his lungs. The mass could not be removed because it was too large. Because the cancer had spread into the lungs, a liver transplant was not an option as the cancer cells in the lungs would attack a transplanted liver. A biopsy would be performed within three days to determine what type of tumor the cancer was. Ethan would need chemotherapy. Angie couldn't stand what she was hearing and had to leave the meeting in which the doctors were conveying this information. She collapsed in the bathroom.

Less than three days later Ethan was put under general anesthetic for a biopsy, which identified the tumor as cancerous, a stage four hepatoblastoma. During the biopsy surgery, a central line was installed into the main arteries in Ethan's chest to prepare for the probability of needing access for treatments. One week after having the biopsy surgery, Ethan began to undergo chemotherapy treatments, in hopes that the tumor would shrink enough to allow for an attempt to remove the cancer surgically.

"I was one of those moms who thought I could never handle losing a child or having a sick child, but when you have to, you just do," Angie said. "Everything was going so well for us, then in one day life completely turned around. It was like a brick hit me." Angie and Cory worked things out so that Angie could be with Ethan all the time. She stayed overnight with him in his hospital bed, not sleeping much for many months, just a couple of hours here and there. The family's life had to revolve around Ethan's treatments—three or four days in the hospital for chemotherapy, then a week "off" at home, two days of which were spent at the hospital. They weren't able to have many people at their home or take Ethan out in public, or even have Mackenzie in preschool due to the risk of a potentially fatal infection. During chemotherapy treatment, Ethan's white blood cell counts would become too low to fight any sort of sickness.

"Your child's sick—you nurture them back to health. That's what a Mom does. But I couldn't," Angie said. "I couldn't take away the pain, the chemotherapy, the horrible tests, the vomitting. I couldn't do anything." On one of the many drives from the cancer treatment centre to her house, Angie wished she could just drive off with Ethan into the sunset in front of them and never have to come back. Many days, Angie stayed at the treatment centre all day with Ethan and Mackenzie, who both came to actually enjoy being at the Cancercare unit with its child-friendly atmosphere. When the nurse told Angie at the beginning of Ethan's treatments that a time would come when Ethan wouldn't want to go home Angie was skeptical, but found she did have a hard time getting her kids to leave after awhile.

Despite the pain and vomitting that Ethan was suffering, he remained a cheerful child throughout the eight months of his treatments. During his first round of chemotherapy he experienced hearing loss at high frequencies and kept throwing up his medications. The tumor shrunk quickly at first, but then it calcified and didn't appear to be shrinking. For a while the mass did not look as though it would become operable. In December, after two months of intense treatment, Angie broke down at the hospital when she realized it could be their last Christmas with Ethan. They decided to get family portraits taken, which hang over their living room mantle now. Ethan has no hair in the portraits but isn't extremely sickly looking. Thankfully, he started off his battle with size on his side and while he didn't gain any weight for a year, he didn't lose any either. The one thing Cory and Angie could get into him was chocolate milk and they would often slip in whipping cream or a thick nutritional drink to try and get his calorie intake up.

Shortly before Christmas, they received the wonderful news that the tumor had shrunk enough to be operable. They continued chemotherapy treatments until surgery, a very risky operation in itself, could be performed in February. The liver has a surface like cottage cheese and bleeds easily and rapidly. A bypass team was brought in to preserve Ethan's life should he begin to lose a lot of blood. Throughout the surgery surgeons kept sending bits of tissue to the lab to test for cancerous cells. After eight hours, they got clear margins in the liver. Ethan came through the surgery extremely well. He needed only one bag of blood for the removal of all of the right lobe and part of the left lobe of his liver as well as his gall bladder.

Angie was waiting outside for Ethan to come out of surgery. She could hear the wheels of his bed coming down the hallway and then the surgeons appeared with tears in their eyes. "The first thing he said was, 'Mommy. I want Mommy,'" they told her. They weren't expecting him to be able to say anything. Ethan was talking and smiling even in the Intensive Care Unit. He came out of surgery very swollen with tubes coming out of his stomach, throat, and nose; but recuperated so rapidly that three days later he was playing and wanting to eat some of the pizza that had been brought in for a Valentine's party.

"I wish that some of these people who are so negative about life would go to the children's oncology unit and see these kids," Angie said. She and Mackenzie befriended a sixteen-year-old boy whose single mother wasn't able to stay with him due to needing to work. They hung out together, and he became a source of information for Angie since Ethan was too young to verbalize what he was going through. Throughout their months at the hospital, Cory and Angie saw many children who didn't make it. During Ethan's last round of chemo, Angie came out of Ethan's room just as staff were taking away the body of a little girl from the room next to Ethan's. As sickening as the sight was for Angie, it served to create a deep appreciation for the fact that she could come back to the hospital for a child who was still alive.

After Ethan's surgery, he still had to continue with chemotherapy for another two months. Then it was another two months of frequent doctor's visits before his central line could be safely removed, a horrible procedure for Ethan to have to endure. Seeing Ethan suffer so much without knowing why was torture for Angie. "I cried every night for probably a year," she said. "People would tell me I was like a rock. They didn't see me crying myself to sleep every night." Ethan would often scream and cry going to sleep, and want to rub Angie's hair for comfort. Her neck felt like it was permanently crooked from leaning over to him at night and during tests. Angie and Cory would try not to cry in front of the children, but sometimes they couldn't hold back their grief. Mackenzie would ask whether Ethan was going to die. Angie would never answer the question but just tell her that they were giving Ethan special medicine to make him better.

At one point, disturbed by all the pain and illness Ethan was enduring, Angie asked the nurses whether they really thought he was going to make it. As much as Angie and Cory wanted to save Ethan, they didn't want to just briefly prolong his life and cause him unnecessary suffering. Even having to change the bandages on Ethan's central line, which Cory had to do at home, would cause little Ethan a lot of stress, and they hated making him scream and cry. Angie needed to know that the treatments were being done for Ethan's sake, not for theirs. The nurses assured her that the treatments were being done to make Ethan better, and that they wouldn't be putting Ethan through chemotherapy and surgery if doctors didn't think he could make it.

Angie's journal in which she recorded Ethan's test results typifies her unswervingly optimistic attitude toward life—bright green with flowers and a yellow smiley face. Inside are notes like "Ate some toast today!", "Complaining of tummy pains. Not sleeping much." "Developed double ear infection", "Very sick with this round of chemo, also had bad cold which contributed to vomitting". There are also a number of Mackenzie's drawings, and evidence of some tic-tac-toe games they played together while spending their days at the hospital with Ethan.

After almost eight months of intense treatments, Ethan's alpha-fetoprotein levels, which measure cancer growth, had gone down to 8. When Ethan was first tested, his level was 250,000. In a cancer-free person, AFP levels are single-digit so an AFP level of 8 was cause for celebration, and cessation of chemotherapy. After Ethan was first released from treatment, he went in for tests every two weeks, then every four, then every three months, and now the interval between visits has been stretched to every six months. "We live six months to six months," Angie says. "I can't sleep a few days before tests and for about a week after while we wait for results." Angie knows the facts—the five-year recurrence rate for Ethan's type of cancer is high, and one of the possible effects of the chemotherapy he had to have is secondary cancer.

"What we had to go through makes you appreciate your children so much," Angie says. Sometimes when she lies beside Ethan at night she still gets a panicky feeling thinking of how close they came to losing him. "How could I cope with losing a child? That was always in the back of my mind. How could I go on? Could I still be a good Mom to Mackenzie?" she asks herself. Angie has also been troubled by trying to figure out why Ethan's cancer happened, feeling like she was being punished even though she was trying her best to be a good mother. She even feels guilt over the development of the cancer, since doctors believe it began to develop while Ethan was still in utero. Despite assurances from doctors and friends that she did and took nothing to cause the cancer, she still somehow feels like the cancer was, in some way, her fault.

It was more than a year after Ethan's treatments ended that Angie's body and mind came out of crisis mode. She was finally able to let her emotional guard down and begin to process all the things that had been building up inside of her. The stark reality of how close they came to losing Ethan really began to hit her. Sometimes she would look at pictures of Ethan in his first two years and wonder, "Was he in pain then?" In addition to processing the past, Angie also had to process the present. Life had become "normal" again and she was so used to revolving around chemotherapy and hospital visits that she had to re-learn how to live a normal lifestyle.

In time, life returned to the wonderful sort of normal that most people take for granted. Angie started up her home daycare again. Mackenzie started school, and Ethan enjoyed playing with the other kids that Angie took care of. Then Angie got what could be medically defined as a surprise. Against the odds of where she was at in her cycle, she got pregnant. When she told Cory what she strongly suspected, he told her, "You couldn't be." But she was. At first, Angie was more afraid than excited. She was horrified at the possibility of "making" another child sick. She also worried about what would happen if Ethan's cancer returned—how could she handle it if she had a baby to look after? After a couple of days of sensing Angie's anxiety, Cory asked his wife, "Can we be excited about this?" Her husband's happiness over the new love that would come into their lives helped Angie to put her fears to rest and become thankful for the unexpected gift of the third child she had always wanted, but been afraid to pursue.

When Angie and Cory sat Mackenzie and Ethan down on the couch to tell them that they would be having a baby brother or sister, Cory started to cry with joy but the kids were not similarly impressed. Ethan thought they should name the baby "poo-head" if it was a boy. It also took some time to convince the kids that they were actually being told the truth. After having some time to get used to the idea, the kids couldn't wait until the day their baby was born by scheduled Caesarean. Mackenzie wanted a baby sister but would tell people she would be happy with either "as long as it's healthy". Angie will always remember the smiles on their faces when they first saw their baby sister Addison, who Angie is now quite positive was "totally meant to be".

Addison is almost a year old now and has quite unintentionally infused new life and great joy into her family. "I look at her as just this little gift," Angie tells me, with two baby girls crawling at her feet, one of which belongs to her best friend. "I know there is a reason she came into our lives." Life has returned to normal at Angie's house, never again to be taken for granted as it is in so many other homes. "It's just a miracle that Ethan is still with us," she realizes. "People say that we should live like every day is a gift. We really do."

On Time and Perspective

Mothers tend to fuss over relatively meaningless things like how often a baby nurses, what foods a toddler won't eat, at what age a child is toilet trained, or what to bring for preschool snack. Sometimes it seems that we let caring for them distract us from caring about them, and from being aware of what the point of caring for them really is.

Over the past couple of years I've been teaching at our church's weekly program for moms. One week I taught on "The Power of Perspective". At that time, I was having somebody from the group read a little something to the women every week since mothers usually spend a lot of time reading to their children but rarely get a chance to read for themselves. That particular week I'd picked a piece by Robin Jones Gunn entitled "What a Mother Says". It humorously recounts a mother's typical phrases to a growing daughter beginning at her birth and ending with, "Don't slip on the rice. Good-bye, honey."[1] I handed it to one of our leaders whose daughter was getting married that summer. She took one look at it and handed it to somebody else to read.

By the time it was read, followed by Rebecca Christian's "A Mother's Letter to a Son Starting Kindergarten", and an unknown author's "To My Grown-Up Son", pretty well all of our leaders were crying. May the tears not fall on deaf ears. May they testify of the need to treasure the moments as they pass, and to make the most of every opportunity we have to be with our children at whatever age they're at.

We so desperately need to learn from people with more perspective than we have. Tragically, and dangerously, respect for older generations has been almost lost in Western societies. While it is certainly true that some free advice is worth exactly what you paid for it, there is also a wealth of wisdom available to us from those who have walked further and longer than we have. What will happen to our society if we continue to forget to remember?

The perspective provided by the passage of time is particularly valuable. As hard as the waiting time was between Tim and Daniel, I can see now that I was being given a gift in the passing of the years. When I look at Tim, I have a built-in reminder of how quickly children change, how fast time passes, and how things tend to appear and disappear in children very rapidly. When Tim went through certain stages that either frustrated or delighted me, the stages seemed like they would be permanent but they wafted away, like the butterflies he has stopped trying to catch. Now, when Daniel goes through the same sorts of stages, I know they will not last and this knowledge both comforts and inspires me. I know he will stop being fixated on the board game he likes so much now. I know he will not always have such small soft hands, such a chirpy little voice, and such a carefree laugh. I know I must drink deeply of the delights of young childhood before they evaporate, and not get ruffled about the little wrinkles that often iron out without any pressure on my part.

Anna Quindlen, a journalist whose children are grown, reflects poignantly on her children's growing-up years. I am planning on writing out the following two lines and putting them up somewhere I'll see them often: "But the biggest mistake I made is the one that most of us make while doing this. I did not live in the moment enough. This is particularly clear now that the moment is gone, captured only in photographs."[2] Why is it that generation after generation of mothers experiences the same sorts of regrets? Why can't we learn from each other when we say these sorts of things? Why do we continue to complain when our children are around, then weep when they leave? Why don't we start to cherish them while we have them so we can smile after they've gone?

On an everyday grocery shopping expedition with both boys I was focused solely on the challenge of capturing food and escaping. As I endured the crawling checkout line I tensely kept an eye on the boys, wriggling haphazardly all around me. Then I remembered reading something an older mother had written, wishing she could spend a day with her two sons. I suddenly stopped just watching my two boys and started to see them—so young, so precious, and so changeable. Even in the short amount of time that has passed since that day they have changed quite a lot. So have I—I can see better now. I am less blind to their beauty.

What seems like a long time ago, I was standing in line at Kentucky Fried Chicken, characteristically focused on getting what I needed and getting going. I was largely oblivious to the three-year-old boy right beside me until a rather rough-looking man looked at him and smiled tenderly. I shouldn't have needed that reminder to notice my own child's preciousness, but that day, my son was just one more thing to look after as I ran from place to place intensely trying to get things arranged for the renovations and move we were about to make. I can barely remember what seemed so important that day.

I don't want to waste these years by wasting these days, by missing the moments that will only come my way once. When we see our children's pictures from the past, our hearts can wring sometimes. Right in front of us we can see an image of the children we once had, but those children in those forms are gone forever. We may long to hold them again, to spend time with them, to cuddle them, to listen to their chatter with new ears, to go back to them—but there is no going back.

We took Daniel in for a medical appointment when he was just twelve days old, tiny and handsome with his Daddy's dark hair. "Enjoy him," a receptionist warned us quite cheerlessly, "They grow up." I know what she was saying about needing to enjoy our little ones because they don't stay little long, but I don't feel that their growing up should end a parents' pleasure in them. While it is true that a newborn baby or a toddler is tenderly cherishable in ways that a ten-year-old or a teenager isn't, I think it is also true that a ten-year-old or a teenager is deep-seatedly precious in ways that a baby or toddler can't yet be. True love has a way of growing instead of wilting.

When Daniel was a baby, he was an escape artist that just wouldn't sit still in shopping carts, or anywhere else for that matter. Things got to the point where I carried around a bungee cord in my purse and had to bungee cord him quite tightly into the cart or risk a certain shopping cart fall. I cannot honestly say I miss the tension of those trips, but I do miss the child. I am starting to run many of my errands alone now and strange as it may sound, I actually miss having someone wriggling around in the cart, someone to pack snacks for, someone to chatter with.

These days, Daniel keeps making little trips up to the computer area, ostensibly to get things he needs like scissors or scrap paper, one piece at a time. He just now snuck up behind me and grabbed the back of my computer chair, trying to get me to try to kiss him before he gets down the stairs with whatever he's pretended to come for. I could tell him to stay downstairs with Daddy and not come up anymore, but I decide not to. I know better now. I know he won't always be so rosy-cheeked and giggly. I know he won't always scamper about, or seek me out for a kiss. I know he won't always be around to bother me.

Thinking about the passage of time can be very heart-wrenching if we are looking back burdened with regrets. I guess that's why I try to look ahead every once in a while—so that I can look back on where I am right now and prevent those regrets. I want to make today something that will bring joy to tomorrow because I know that whatever I plant is what I will harvest, and whatever direction I move toward is the destination I will eventually arrive at.

Sometimes when we are up to our eyeballs in laundry, dishes, and diapers it is easy to lose sight of the fact that we are going somewhere. However, we need to keep in mind that all of us are on an extremely important journey, and our children are following our lead. We were made for something great—not a treadmill, nor a racetrack—but for a path that leads to life. One step at a time we journey into eternity, and there is no going back.

Lara's Story

Lara and Jeff suffered several losses in their first few years of married life. Lara's father was diagnosed with lung cancer shortly after their wedding and died four months later. His death was followed rapidly by several other difficult deaths on both sides of their family. After three years of grief, the couple was thrilled to have a bright spot in their lives—a baby to look forward to. The pregnancy had happened just as they'd planned, after they both had gotten settled into their pharmaceutical careers. Lara felt great, the ultrasounds were perfect, and there were no pregnancy-related problems in her family.

Then one evening, when she was less than twenty-four weeks into her pregnancy, Lara began to feel as though she may be having contractions. Lara and Jeff went to the hospital to ask what was going on, but were sent home. As Lara climbed back into bed at home, her water broke. They went back to the hospital, where staff tried to stave off delivery for at least forty-eight hours in order to have enough time to administer drugs that would hastily speed up the baby's lung development. At that time, babies born at 24 weeks gestation had less than one percent chance of surviving and being normal. Their odds of just surviving were not much higher.

Doctors were unable to keep the baby inside Lara's body for enough time to be able to administer sufficient lung development dosage to give the baby any chance to be able to breathe in the outside world. Cassandra Marie was born weighing one pound five ounces. She was placed into Lara's arms and came out of the delivery room alive, breathing only every once in a while. She lived for over two hours, then passed away while Lara was passed out from all the drugs in her system. Cassandra was born just before midnight and died at two in the morning in her father's arms. Lara was sent home that day with a pamphlet entitled "Because We Care". When she went to bed that night, utterly exhausted, it hit her. There was no movement and no baby. She wasn't pregnant anymore, but she didn't have a baby. The baby was gone, just gone. Months of hopes and dreams and plans completely disappeared within a matter of hours.

Lara looks through a small wooden memory box as she tells me her story, looking for more evidence of this little life, but she doesn't have much to hold on to. She opens up a piece of paper and I can read a big bright red stamp through the onionskin paper: "DECEASED". The heartlessness of it disturbs me. The main item inside the box is a smaller than doll-sized crocheted yellow outfit. I can hardly imagine a baby small enough to wear it, but when Lara shows me the picture of Cassandra wearing it, it is huge on her. I ask Lara who made it and she says she doesn't know, explaining that there is a group of women who knit for the neo-natal unit at the hospital "so the mothers will have something".

Then Lara finds a calendar that she used as her pregnancy journal and flips through it. "Jeff felt the baby move today," she reads, then looks up. "One week later we were having a funeral." They buried their tiny daughter beside Lara's father on a bleak March day. "It was cold, very cold," Lara remembers. Then there was nothing to do but go back to work, where she was met with a different sort of coldness. Because people didn't seem to know what to say, most said nothing.

Doctors told the couple that what had happened was a fluke, that it was nothing to worry about, and that they should try and get pregnant again right away. So a few months after losing Cassandra they found themselves pregnant again, taking comfort in the assurances that everything would be fine this time. Lara enjoyed another perfect pregnancy, until one evening close to Christmas when she felt like she lost her mucous plug. She was twenty-four weeks along. "Not again," Lara thought.

This time when they went to the hospital the nurses noticed that her membranes were bulging and she was brought to another hospital where she remained for a week and a half lying on alternate sides, receiving frequent injections in her hips. She would repeatedly start to bleed profusely, upsetting one nurse in particular who wasn't very reassuring. "Look at what's happening to you," she half-yelled at Lara, showing her a blood-soaked bed pad. "They should be doing something about this. We don't have enough staff to deal with this."

Sometimes Lara would call Jeff in the middle of the night to tell him she was hemorrhaging again. She felt helpless, frustrated, and devastated, realizing there was absolutely nothing she could do to keep her baby inside of her. She lived in constant tension, frightfully aware that if her child was born it had very little chance of surviving. After Lara's membranes had been bulging for quite some time, her uterus became infected and she began to develop a dangerously high fever. However, due to an anti-labor drug she had been receiving, the severity of her fever was masked. Lara's body was beginning to turn septic.

Jeff was able to stay overnight at the hospital on Christmas Eve. Very early Christmas morning Lara said to him, "I need a blanket. I'm cold." When Jeff felt his wife, cold and shaking violently, he knew something was seriously wrong and went to get a nurse. Doctors quickly decided Lara's condition was serious and they had no choice but to take the baby. As Lara was being prepared for an emergency caesarean she and Jeff were asked whether or not they wanted any measures taken to save their baby. Unable to imagine people saying no to that question, they signed the forms for "heroic measures". Jeff was sent to a waiting room to wait, horribly aware he could lose both his wife and his child. Lara lay alone in the operating room, listening to staff take inventory of everything they needed to cut her open. Then they put her under.

When Lara came to she saw Jeff sitting beside her. "She's alive. It's a girl," he told her. Lara insisted on seeing their baby and she was wheeled the long way from her ward to the neo-natal intensive care unit. Everything was surreal for Lara, her body and emotions traumatized by fever, drugs, fear and stress. By that point her body was septic and she passed out when she got to where Miranda Faith was being cared for. Miraculously, Baby Miranda remained alive despite all the odds against her. Since her birth was able to be postponed long enough to administer the lung development drugs as well as giving her an extra critical week of development, she was born an ounce and a half heavier than Cassandra was just nine months earlier.

Doctors told the couple their baby would probably not survive, but Jeff and Lara fervently hoped and prayed that the doctors were wrong. With each passing day their hopes rose. Just four days after surgery Lara checked herself out of the hospital even though she was still far too ill to be alone. She had already been in the hospital for what seemed like ages and she simply could not stand being on the maternity floor where everyone had a baby but her and where all she could hear was crying babies. To make her situation even more difficult to bear, Lara's roommate was completely uninterested in her child. "Your baby needs feeding," the nurses would tell her.

"You feed it," the roommate would reply.

Lara told Jeff she wanted to leave. He didn't have the heart to tell her she couldn't go home so he deferred to the doctors, figuring they would never let her leave. The next day, Lara signed everything she needed to sign in order to check herself out against medical advice, and then phoned Jeff to tell him to pick her up. He hit the roof, but took her home, where she was unable to even get out of bed without Jeff's help. Lara took a long time to recover from everything her body had been through but she still tried to get to the hospital every day to see her baby even though she didn't have a vehicle to drive. Friends or relatives would drive Lara to the hospital to spend time beside Miranda, whom she couldn't touch. In the evenings, Jeff and Lara would go together to see their tiny daughter.

Miranda lived from Christmas Day all the way to New Year's, and then on into January, one intense day at a time. Lara kept a journal of Miranda's medical developments and felt full of hope for their daughter. She recorded Miranda getting off a blood pressure drug, coming down on her respirator, beginning to eat a little, and turning from transparent to a more pinkish white sort of color. Her entry for January 16th says, "Doing well. Had a good night. Gained 20 grams… I can't wait for my precious little one to come home perfectly healthy." After several weeks, Lara received a phone call from a hospital psychologist who had been contacted by one of the nurses. The nurse thought Lara was too calm about things. She didn't feel Lara was connected to reality in believing that her daughter would live and called for a psychologist to "help her deal with reality". Lara felt betrayed. The nurses in the unit became like family to the parents who came to be near their children every day, and Lara had felt safe there. Lara told the psychologist that she didn't care what people thought and if she needed him she would call him.

On January 25th, Miranda's one-month birthday, Lara's journal reads, "Now weighs 720 grams. She is doing great. She has started to put her fingers in her mouth and on her lips and the nurse said she's started to move the fluid out of her lungs by herself." They held a 30-day celebration at the hospital that evening. The next morning, Miranda died.

Jeff and Lara were at church early that morning when they got the news. "I can remember the exact spot I was standing," she told me, "I just crumpled into a ball on the floor and started sobbing." An elder came and put his arms around her and it felt to Lara like he took on some of her grief. He began to weep and her own overpowering grief was relieved. Another elder took Jeff and Lara to the hospital where they held their second baby girl before they had to let her go. Then they had another funeral, and buried another baby beside her grandfather. Lara displayed pictures of Miranda from her birth until her one-month celebration. The funeral was much bigger this time and Lara remembers thinking that Miranda touched more lives in her thirty days than many people do in a lifetime.

Jeff and Lara received a plaster imprint of Miranda's tiny hands and feet from the hospital. One hand was curled outward a little and when he saw the plaque Jeff said, "I can still hold her hand." They keep it close by in their kitchen but don't show it to many people. On her desk at work Lara has Cassandra's footprints on a printed piece of paper with an inscription underneath—"In Everything Give Thanks."

I asked Lara if she felt any anger at God, any doubt in Him after being so sure that Miranda would make it. "The best way to describe it is that God just picked me up and held me until I didn't need it anymore. There was such peace in it. I still had pain but I was sheltered, covered, loved. It was the most phenomenal experience." People around her were angry, demanding to know why God would let Miranda die. Jeff and Lara were told some horrible things insinuating that they must have done something to allow Satan to attack them, that they must have done something for God to punish them, or that they didn't pray hard enough.

Lara thought these insinuations through and was wise enough not to take them into her heart. "Even now, I don't know why Miranda died. It's not that I don't care. I just don't think God has to tell me the reasons why. Is it fair? Absolutely not. Is He still God? Oh yeah. And He's caring for them. It's not like I'll never see them again. I never went, 'God, how could you?' God is God. Who am I to question Him? He doesn't owe me anything. Children are a gift."

Lara took six weeks off of work to grieve, not just for one but for two babies, since she hadn't really been able to grieve for Cassandra yet. She found herself "wondering if I was ever going to be a mother. Actually, I shouldn't say that. I was a mother. I was wondering if I could ever keep one." She packed away the baby stuff she had gathered and went back to work, where people were again at a loss as to what to say. One large male colleague greeted her with an enormous hug, dissolving her immediately into tears. In some ways she feels she should have taken more time off work, but didn't know what else to do with herself. She knew it wouldn't be good for her to continue to be home alone all day, but wasn't entirely prepared to deal with that many people again.

Lara became a medical interest case. Nobody could explain why the same thing had happened to her twice. Lara and Jeff avoided pregnancy for a year, simply unable to deal with the possibility of going through the grief again. Then they suffered two or three early miscarriages, one of which occurred during a family gathering, another of which appeared to be twins, before becoming pregnant with a pregnancy that went beyond eight weeks. Lara took medical leave and went on bed rest. At fifteen weeks she had surgery to stitch together the opening of her cervix, a procedure that carried a risk of miscarriage. The baby did survive the procedure and Lara stayed on bed rest, getting up only once a day to eat supper. For a total of eighteen weeks she lay on her side and lost twenty-six pounds. She would feel faint when she would get up to shower on a stool that Jeff would set up in the bathroom for her.

Then again, unbelievably and in spite of her sacrificial precautions, Lara lost her mucous plug at twenty-four weeks. She was brought to the hospital and laid in an inclined bed for three days, receiving drugs that made her feel quite convinced that her ice chips were a ham and cheese sandwich. A decision was made to take the baby before Lara became dangerously infected again, and another caesarean was performed, this time with Lara awake. She had been in labor so long that the uterus was gripping onto the baby's head and another incision had to be made in order to safely remove the head. Lara saw a little hand in a bassinet before the baby was taken away but didn't know whether it belonged to a boy or a girl. She was surprised when she found out it was a boy, two pounds and one half of an ounce, significantly and unaccountably heavier than his sisters at the same gestation.

Shortly after delivery, Michael Ryan developed an irreparable major brain bleed. Doctors told Jeff and Lara that if their baby lived he would have severe brain damage. When Lara woke up in the middle of Michael's first night, there was a neonatal doctor standing at the foot of her bed. Lara felt her heart sink but the doctor was only there to ask permission to give the baby a blood transfusion, as babies that early don't make their own blood. Miraculously, by the next time the baby's brain bleed was assessed, it had completely disappeared. Michael lived precariously. Jeff and Lara went daily to be with their son, hoping and praying fervently for his survival. When Michael was twelve days old, Lara felt like she could begin a journal for him.

Dear Michael,

I decided today was the day to start a journal for you. You have not had the best night so the nurses are watching you closely. Daddy prayed over you last night. He said, "Michael there is power in the hand of God. Tonight the hand of God will touch you."… Daddy just phoned up to the NICU and they took you off of the paralyzing drug and you have not spasmed again. When I look at you I see God working. When things look scary all I hear from God is "Trust Me." So, Michael, I have put your life in God's hands. It is not always easy to leave you there but I know God has great plans for your life and He is the only one who can save your life.… I love you, Michael! Love Mom.

On Michael's sixteenth day, Jeff wrote this to his tiny son:

I called the NICU this morning. Apparently you didn't have such a good night again last night…

Michael, more than anything I want you to come home. My heart yearns for the day when you and I can play catch, when you can teach me how to fish (I'm terrible at it), when we can go to a football game together, when we can pray together. At this moment, I can't imagine anything I wouldn't do for you. And we don't even really know each other yet but that doesn't matter because I will always love you because you are my son. My love for you is not dependent on whether you are successful or not, or smart or not, or handsome or not. My love for you is not dependent on anything except this – that you are my son—and that will never change. If you listen to nothing else I say, do this—seek God, run after Him and never stop. He is worth everything!!

Underneath this entry Jeff wrote this verse—

Light arises in the darkness for the upright. PSALM 112:4

That very day the hospital called, again while Jeff and Lara were at church on a Sunday, and told them Michael was dying and that there was nothing they could do. The situation was horribly reminiscent of the Sunday morning that Miranda died. This time, they went home together first, where they prayed and took communion together. They were as ready as they could be to let go—again. By the time they got to the hospital, Michael had turned around, with no medically perceivable explanation.

After that, Michael's health continued to improve inch by inch. When Michael was six weeks old, they got to hold him for the first time. Lara is glowing in that picture—the first time she ever got to hold a baby that had any hope of living. Almost two months after Michael's birth Lara wrote, "Today is my birthday and I got the greatest gift. We started breastfeeding today." Though she struggled valiantly to make nursing work, Michael was just too small and weak to be able to nurse properly. His hand covered only the tip of her index finger. Jeff's wedding ring could fit around Michael's wrist.

After fourteen weeks in the hospital, it looked as if Michael was almost ready to be able to come home, but then he needed to have eye surgery as he was born with his eyes fused shut. This was a frustrating setback, as was his inoculation at three months, but after fifteen weeks in the hospital, Michael Ryan was able to come home to stay, still early for his due date. Not only has Michael survived the overwhelming odds against just being alive, but he miraculously has no complications associated with such premature birth—no eyesight problems, no asthma, and no learning disabilities. During his babyhood, Michael was about four months behind in development. At his first birthday party, Lara said, "He just sat there. No teeth. He wasn't walking. We didn't care as long as he was here."

Michael is eight years old now. While Lara and I are talking in their front room he comes in to kiss his Mommy goodnight dressed in his dinosaur pajamas, then has some cheese for a night snack.

"He's a walking stomach," Lara tells me, clearly delighted in him. Michael has been curious about his sisters lately and once told her, "I don't think that's fair. They get to be with Jesus and I have to stay down here." She told him she really wanted him to stay here with her.

What Lara went through on her road to motherhood serves as an almost-constant reminder to put the challenges and frustrations of child raising into perspective, like Michael's recent habit of almost always forgetting his lunch-kit or his homework at school. "He wasn't supposed to ever be able to go to school, or even walk--so what if he forgets his lunch-kit?" Lara reminds herself.

Lara always wanted a large family, but finds herself very satisfied with having just Michael. Sometimes Lara is asked why they don't have more children. She finds that question difficult to answer, but not as difficult as being accused of being selfish for having only one child. As doctors couldn't name or fix whatever was causing Lara's body to birth babies at twenty-four weeks, Jeff and Lara decided that she would have her tubes tied. They simply could not put another child through the intense pain and suffering that premature babies have to experience.

When Michael was just two weeks old, long before Jeff knew whether or not his son would live, he wrote this to him—

Never give up on God, Michael. Always follow after Him with all your heart, all your passion, all your strength. Never be afraid to be brutally honest with Him but always be ready for the loving correction and discipline He will provide. God bless you tonight, Michael.

Chapter Seven

To Be

Journal Entries

September 7th

Daniel started kindergarten today. I locked myself out of the house when I went out with the boys to wait for the bus. I'm chalking this up to being severely short on sleep, and am grateful for a nice neighbor who let me use her cell phone to call Herb even though she was running late for work.

Lying in bed at night I felt thankful that Daniel seems to like his teacher, seems to like school, and seems to be moving toward making friends. I felt deep, sweet joy in motherhood, grateful to be a mother to these two boys, and also felt strongly that I did not want to be done with Mommying. I want another First Day of School.

September 9th

Came home to a surprise a few days ago. My neighbor-writer-friends Brenda and Duncan had their baby two weeks early. Tim came around to the back yard where I was hanging out with Daniel and told me Brenda and Duncan were in our front yard with a baby. Sure enough, there they were with a brand-new black-haired baby girl—so tiny and beautiful, so much like our little Daniel. They've named her Katya. I don't know whether seeing these sorts of things is good for me or not.

September 10th

Daniel gets to sit in the back of the bus with his big brother, a privilege seldom granted to a kindergartener. Tim had to move back by stages, having earned the back-of-the-bus privilege now by being in fifth grade, the oldest grade in their school. Daniel looks so cute back there with the big kids, wearing his orange jacket and red backpack, quite perky and cheery. On the way home, however, (he comes home at 11:30, Tim at 3:30) he sits in the very front seat. They all do. Six small kindergarteners in one big bus and they all pack in the front two seats, like little ducklings.

September 16th

Stood out on the sidewalk this morning with the boys watching Tim try to make fire using a magnifying glass and some newspaper. I didn't think this would really work, but he did get some flames going. One of our neighbors came by with her new nine-week-old, hyper puppy. I mentioned something about it being like having another baby. She said quite definitively that she was all done with that. She has two almost-adult boys that she pretends not to be crazy about, one of which is named Daniel. "My Daniel is buying a car today," she tells my Daniel, or probably me, "and it wasn't long since he was your size."

September 26th

Got the stomach flu rather violently last night and felt so weak so quickly. Made me feel very uninterested in doing sixteen weeks of nausea and vomitting again.

September 27th

Phoned home tonight. Mom was sick with the stomach flu (couldn't have got it from me since we live four hours apart) and had gone to bed, but it was a good night to talk with Dad. The volunteer fire department was burning Oma's house down. I hadn't known anything about this, but I guess Dad had decided after getting the last tax bill that it wasn't wise to hold onto the house for sentimental purposes, especially since he wasn't able to get any decent renters. There was no proper heat or water and the house was often full of bugs, rodents, or reptiles, but it had been home to Dad. Apparently, the house used to be a small barn, then it housed an entire family of eleven (some children slept in the bathroom), before taking in my father's family after they immigrated in 1953. To be honest, I will miss the house too, but nothing on earth lasts forever.

October 3rd

Well, today is D-day and I am getting conflicting reports from my body. I am just going to have to wait it out and prepare for anything. Unbelievably, I am still feeling like I would like more time before getting pregnant. I am under a lot of stress right now and don't feel ready to do this well yet. Yesterday there was a devotional in my Bible beside the account of the miraculous conception of John the Baptist, one sentence of which I found particularly timely:

"Elizabeth's comprehension of the high value of a new life, and of the perfection of God's timing, gave her the ability to rest in His perfect plan and made her the ideal mother." [1]

October 4th

Visited the evening mom's group tonight. Lisa said something about Michael coming into her room in the middle of the night with nightmares and her telling him it was his own fault for watching something he wasn't supposed to watch on TV. A friend of hers from work tells us affectionately, "Oh, Lisa pretends to be so tough. She's just a big softie."

"We know," I tell her.

October 5th

There is a very real possibility that I am pregnant. I am several days late now and feeling very different. Lisa emailed me today to say she was worried about me because I looked dreadfully tired last night, which I am.

Went to the park for a brief slice of time to try to prepare for this possibility in between working for the afternoon and attending an evening meeting. Didn't eat before I left so I bought myself two different ice creams for supper, just in case I'm eating for two. This could be it. This could really be it.

October 6th

This isn't it.

October 10th

Was reading an article on busyness in a women's magazine. One of the women interviewed wondered how she was going to have time to fit her baby into her life. She knew in her heart that she had a wrong attitude and wanted to change it, just like I do.

When I was pretty sure last week that I was pregnant, I was trying to muster up excitement, but the stress and fatigue from miscellaneous things going on made me feel like I was internally yelling, "Wait!" I want to be able to welcome and care for a child with my whole heart.

October 15th

Have been hearing reports of Barb and Jon's new baby Annabelle needing surgery for something that is wrong with her skull. I will have to email them.

October 16th

Went shopping with Tim today for a birthday present for Daniel. I saw really nice Christmas stockings, which I've been hoping to find for quite some time. I picked out four, then realized I should really buy five just in case. I landed up buying six—I have always wanted four children.

October 18th

Daniel is five years old today. I am so happy to have him. I took little muffins into his kindergarten class, where I was informed that he didn't want to wear his birthday crown. When I went into the office to sign in the secretary asked, "Somebody's birthday?" I made some sort of standard comment about kids growing up quickly and she shook her head sort of sadly. "My oldest is eighteen already," she told me, "and it seems like just yesterday that I was doing this," indicating my container of messy cupcakes.

October 21st

Had a little birthday party for Daniel tonight—just two friends but the three of them made enough noise and mess to suggest a much larger affair.

October 25th

Got an email from Jon in response to my asking about little Annabelle's surgery. What she needed was surgery to reposition the bone above her left eye. Doctors cut out and completely removed a piece of her skull, reshaped it, then rotated it 180 degrees from its original position before sewing it back in. Her incision goes over the top of her head from ear to ear. Poor baby!

Jon wrote, "Being in the intensive care unit readjusts your perspective. We saw a fourteen-year-old who had brain surgery to remove a tumor, and a twelve-year-old who had heart surgery that went wrong and he ended up with a stroke. He can't talk. I was all worked up about this relatively routine procedure and I now see how much worse things could have been. I have so much to be thankful for."

October 26th

Went to Brenda's book launch tonight. The place was packed. My friend and I just barely got the last seats at the last minute. Brenda came by, long hair flowing, to greet people. "Superstar!" I exclaimed.

"Oh, my parents know a lot of people," she said. Brenda is remarkably modest.

The family table was rather cluttered with kids and their things. Katya's car seat sat on the table. Katya herself, dark and tiny, was with one grandmother, Sebastian with the other. A number of other children bounced about.

"I bought this skirt a long time ago and didn't have anywhere to wear it, so thanks for giving me the chance to get out," she told the audience. "I just barely squeezed it on tonight." What must it be like to launch a baby and a book at the same time? Each in themselves is an all-consuming venture.

The moment Brenda finished her reading and walked away from the podium, Sebastian reached out his arms to her. "Ma-ma," I could hear him say across the room. Brenda went straight to him and took him in her arms.

October 27th

Phoned my little nephew, Fletcher, for his one-year-old birthday. He had just gotten up from his nap but did say, "Guh," after I wished him a happy birthday and asked how he was doing. Daniel says Fletcher was saying, "Good."

Realized this morning that today is exactly a year since my surgery. Was reading in Genesis this morning about Sarah having Isaac after so many years of waiting and a verse caught my eye—"It all happened at the time God had said it would."[2]

Epilogue

So here we are at the end of a book that I originally thought was going to chronicle the journey of having a baby. After three years and almost sixty thousand words, I am still waiting, and wondering.

For some time now I have been wondering how and when to end this book.

I was reading a good article on endings in a writers' magazine a while ago titled "Bad Wraps".[1] The columnist listed five types of endings that should be avoided at all costs because they are anticlimactic. One he called "The Deflator"—a "never mind" sort of thing. We are also supposed to avoid "The Surprise", "The Detour", "The Meander", and "The Sudden Stop", with the caveat that if we have no natural ending we have to work in clues that this is indeed the end. So, if being at the back of the book didn't tip you off, this is indeed the end—for now. I actually feel like the end of this book might be more like a beginning.

"Humans," the columnist stated, "have a built-in need for conclusion."[2] I agree wholeheartedly but the thing is, humans usually don't look far enough ahead when we're searching for or drawing conclusions. If you're writing a novel, or anything in which you get to sort of control what happens in the story, who's in it, who dies, who doesn't, and how the story ends; you can avoid the anticlimactic conclusions. But it doesn't work that way in real life. Real life is full of all five "bad wraps"—deflators, surprises, detours, sudden stops, and meanders.

But isn't it a miracle how everything will work out in the end?

Endnotes

Chapter 1

[1] Adrienne Rich, *Of Woman Born: Motherhood as Experience and Institution* (New York: W. W. Norton, 1986), p.39.

[2] I Samuel 1:8, NIV

Chapter 2

[1] Anna Quindlen, *Loud and Clear* (New York: Random House, 2004), back cover.

Chapter 3

[1] Julie Ann Barnhill, *She's Gonna Blow: Real Help for Moms Dealing with Anger* (Eugene: Harvest House, 2005).

Chapter 4

[1] Frances J. Roberts, *Come Away My Beloved* (Uhrichsville: Barbour Publishing, 2002), p. 17.

[2] Ibid., p. 18.

[3] Ibid., p. 186.

Chapter 5

[1] Roberts, p. 254.

[2] Roberts, p. 269.

[3] Sheri Rose Shepherd, *Prayers to My King* (Sisters: Multnomah Publishers, 2005), p. 140.

[4] Horatio Spafford, "It is Well with my Soul", 1873.

[5] Sheri Rose Shepherd, *His Princess: Love Letters from your King* (Sisters: Multnomah Publishers, 2004), p. 96.

[6] May Sarton, *At Eighty-Two* (New York: W.W. Norton, 1996), p. 181.

Chapter 6

[1] Robin Jones Gunn, "What a Mother Says", in *Mothering by Heart* (Sisters: Multnomah Publishers, 1996).

[2] Anna Quindlen, *Loud and Clear* (New York: Random House, 2004), p. 10-11.

Chapter 7

[1] Jeanne Hendricks, "The Legacy of Elizabeth" in Elisa Morgan, ed. *Mom's Devotional Bible* (Grand Rapids: Zondervan Publishing House, 1996), p. 1147.

[2] Genesis 21:2, NLT

Epilogue

[1] David A. Fryxell, "Bad Wraps" in *Writer's Digest*, May 2005, Volume 8, No. 5.

[2] Ibid., p. 24.

Visit the author on her website:
Elizabethadam.com

Or write her at:

Elizabeth Adam
21 Deer Lodge Place
Winnipeg, Manitoba, Canada
R3J 2B6

Also available:

Great Expectation: An Inspirational Pregnancy Companion

Mother Love would make an excellent gift for your Moms group.

Order online at Elizabethadam.com or mail the following form to the address above:

ORDER FORM	QUANTITY
Mother Love: Portraits of its Power	
Great Expectation: An Inspirational Pregnancy Companion	

NAME:______________________________

PHONE: ______________ EMAIL: ______________

ADDRESS:______________________________

CITY: ______________ STATE/PROV: ______________

ZIP/POSTAL CODE______________________